SOCIAL PEDAGOGY AND SOCIAL WORK

SOCIAL PEDAGOGY AND SOCIAL WORK

LOWIS CHARFE AND ALI GARDNER

Los Angeles | London | New Delhi
Singapore | Washington DC | Melbourne

Los Angeles | London | New Delhi
Singapore | Washington DC | Melbourne

SAGE Publications Ltd
1 Oliver's Yard
55 City Road
London EC1Y 1SP

SAGE Publications Inc.
2455 Teller Road
Thousand Oaks, California 91320

SAGE Publications India Pvt Ltd
B 1/l 1 Mohan Cooperative Industrial Area
Mathura Road
New Delhi 110 044

SAGE Publications Asia-Pacific Pte Ltd
3 Church Street
#10-04 Samsung Hub
Singapore 049483

Editor: Kate Keers
Assistant editor: Talulah Hall
Production editor: Martin Fox
Copyeditor: Jane Fricker
Proofreader: Christine Bitten
Indexer: Gary Kirby
Marketing manager: Samantha Glorioso
Cover design: Wendy Scott
Typeset by: C&M Digitals (P) Ltd, Chennai, India
Printed in the UK

Library of Congress Control Number: 2018958643

British Library Cataloguing in Publication data

A catalogue record for this book is available from the
British Library

Activate Learning

ISBN 978-1-5264-4205-5
ISBN 978-1-5264-4206-2 (pbk)

At SAGE we take sustainability seriously. Most of our products are printed in the UK using responsibly sourced
papers and boards. When we print overseas we ensure sustainable papers are used as measured by the PREPS
grading system. We undertake an annual audit to monitor our sustainability.

CONTENTS

ABOUT THE AUTHORS

Lowis Charfe is a Senior Lecturer at the University of Central Lancashire and is the Course Leader for the BA (Hons) in Social Pedagogy, Advocacy and Participation and joint Course Leader for the MA in Social Pedagogy Leadership. Alongside teaching she has run various training sessions around social pedagogy for several local authority teams and third sector organisations. She is also the lead for the UK partner team in the Erasmus funded Massive Open On-Line Course (MOOC) project, Social Pedagogy in Europe. Headed by ThemPra, the project has developed a short online course looking at the role of social pedagogy across Europe. She also sits on the Board of Trustees for the Social Pedagogy Professional Association and supported the development of the Standards of Proficiency in Social Pedagogy and the Standards for Education and Training. Before joining the university Lowis worked as a qualified social worker in a Leaving Care Team, supporting young care leavers and her first role after qualifying was as a Youth Offending Team Officer for the Manchester YOT service.

Ali Gardner is a Senior Lecturer at the University of Central Lancashire (UCLan) and is joint Course Leader for the MA in Social Pedagogy Leadership. She teaches on a number of programmes including social work and social pedagogy. Ali qualified as a social worker in 1993 and has worked predominantly with adults with a learning disability. Over this time she has developed educational resources and published books relating to personalisation, choice and control. Ali has been the Director of an Advocacy Project working with children and adults for over 10 years. Ali first became interested in social pedagogy when she joined UCLan in 2014 seeing many of the concepts applicable within her own work and value base. Ali is currently working closely with a number of local authorities and adult social care providers to develop the understanding and application of social pedagogy in working alongside adults.

ABOUT THE CONTRIBUTOR

Lindy Simpson is a freelance social work consultant and lecturer who provides academic teaching and practice-based training with a focus on relational participation within the statutory and voluntary child and family and mental health sectors. She currently teaches on the BA (Hons) Social Pedagogy, Advocacy and Participation degree and is an Associate Director of the Centre for Children and Young People's Participation at the University of Central Lancashire. She is a member of the facilitating team developing the MOOC project, Social Pedagogy in Europe. Lindy was previously a senior lecturer at UClan and prior to that she led on the development of regional inpatient CAMHS services for the NHS where she received the national award from Positive Practice in Mental Health for making a difference to mental health services. Lindy also led on the development and implementation of the Independent Review Service for Cumbria County Council and held the position of Children's Rights Officer where she managed advocacy and participation.

FOREWORD

TOWARDS A SOCIAL PEDAGOGICAL PERSPECTIVE ON SOCIAL WORK

GABRIEL EICHSTELLER AND SYLVIA HOLTHOFF, THEMPRA SOCIAL PEDAGOGY CIC

There is little doubt that social work is one of the most important professions. By identifying and addressing the social inequalities, which originate from human interactions and social constructs, it fulfils a core function within society. If the key to understanding any society is how it treats its most disadvantaged members, then the status and focus of social work tell us a lot. Given the increasing pressures experienced by social work teams as austerity continues to exacerbate many people's struggles, it has never been more necessary to strengthen social workers.

At the same time, there are also encouraging signs that the tide is turning, that new opportunities for radical change are arising. It is our collective and individual task to bring about a sea change by making a positive case for relationship-centred practice that enhances people's well-being, increases their resourcefulness and supports their inclusion into wider society. Based on our experience of supporting professionals on their social pedagogy journeys over the last 12 years, we believe that social pedagogy can help inspire sustainable change, which means not just reverting back to how social work used to be a generation ago but rethink, reclaim and reinvent social work in the 21st century. More importantly than our beliefs, however, are experiences in practice, where many professionals have led the way in underpinning their social work practice with a social pedagogical perspective.

This book puts this vision forward, arguing convincingly for a close relationship between social pedagogy and social work. Written by esteemed authors who know the field of social work inside out both as practitioners and lecturers at the largest School of Social Work in the country, this book offers a unique and hugely valuable perspective. It demonstrates how social pedagogy can enhance social work practice, celebrating what's great about social work whilst also setting new impulses to change the system. It showcases this synergy in concrete and practice-relevant ways and thus succeeds in outlining how a social pedagogical perspective can support social workers, particularly in reappraising the importance of relationship-centred practice and challenging some of the suspicions preventing social workers from developing positive, authentic and trusting relationships with the people they support.

Relationships have always been at the heart of social work, which is why social pedagogy should feel familiar, perhaps at first sight even like the Emperor's new clothes. To us this sense of familiarity is an important starting point in exploring the relationship between social pedagogy and social work. But it is equally important to go beyond the familiar, to change one's frame of reference and look for points of differences and opportunities for learning. In most countries, social pedagogy is not synonymous with social work, and for important reasons. A social pedagogical perspective seeks to draw attention to social justice issues and to enable professionals to critically reflect upon, and stay tuned into, the structural factors that cause social inequality rather than blame individuals for the hardship and challenges they encounter. Professionals must mediate between the individuals, groups or communities they support and wider society, which means that they need to think about relationships not just in terms of professional–client relationships but of how they can effectively nurture people's interdependence.

This perspective is not only important in social work. Indeed, we think that social pedagogy has far greater relevance, for instance as a perspective within early years, education, youth work, the justice system, community support and elderly care. For this reason, we hope that it can help counter the segmentation of practice areas and instead connect professionals involved in different aspects of an individual, group or family's life. Its integrative potential lies in resonating deeply with a broad range of professionals who are determined to resist the medicalisation and pathologisation of social care in favour of a more developmental orientation, an educational approach that builds on human potential, resourcefulness and resilience.

We are convinced that this book will make an important contribution to an open and lively discussion about the future of social work and the potential to forge new alliances with related professions. It should therefore be read by other professional groups too, so that other practice fields will recognise the possibilities that a social pedagogical perspective could offer and how this could underpin the practices of early years professionals, youth workers, educators, prison and probation officers, community support workers, and carers for older people, to name just a few fields. Most importantly though, we hope that by reading this book you'll gain new ideas of how you can make even more of a difference in the lives of the people you support.

ACKNOWLEDGEMENTS

We would like to dedicate this book to Jo Cunningham whose belief and support has allowed us to undertake this social pedagogical journey. Always leading from the front with true social pedagogical values and a big smile on her face, she will always be at the heart of everything we do.

We would also like to thank Jane Lloyd who helped us discover social pedagogy and paved the way for all the developments here at the University of Central Lancashire.

Thank you to Lindy Simpson for contributing her excellent chapter on Participation and making sure that the principles were embedded throughout the book.

A special thanks to Gabriel Eichsteller and Sylvia Holthoff and everybody at ThemPra for their continued support and guidance.

Finally, a special thanks to our families and friends who are now fully versed in social pedagogy and available for training.

Lowis and Ali

INTRODUCTION

LOWIS CHARFE AND ALI GARDNER

As social work academics with experience of working with children and adults, we became interested in social pedagogy as we identified the connections with the humanistic values and motivations leading us to our roles. We hope as you read this book you will begin to recognise these connections and share our enthusiasm for this way of working. As part of our role, we have had the opportunity to talk to many students and practitioners working in social care and social work about social pedagogy. We often see that moment of recognition when they begin to understand what it is. This is because they can link the philosophy, theory and concepts to social work practice. Person-centred practice is a good example of this as it fits with key social pedagogical concepts of working alongside people, just one of the ideas we are going to explain further in this book. As with social work, social pedagogy is based on humanistic values and a sense and drive of wanting to help make a difference in people's lives and wider society. As such it is a vocational, philosophical and a holistic approach to life on a personal and professional level.

Social pedagogy has a rich and varied history throughout Europe and South America and there are many key thinkers that have developed and enriched social pedagogical practice, which we explore in Chapter 2. Social pedagogy started out as a philosophical debate aimed at exploring the promotion of social justice and equality within societies and supporting individuals to gain self-confidence and self-efficacy to solve problems they faced. Key historical thinkers began to challenge the ideology and practice of educational systems and develop social pedagogical principles. These principles and philosophy became embedded into wider culture and social pedagogical values have been adopted in practice throughout Europe.

Within Europe and South America, social pedagogy is embedded into the culture and practice within social work, social care and educational settings. It has a broader social function than social work practice and has a wider application. For instance in Germany social pedagogues work within a wide range of public services from early years, statutory social work services to community-based projects. In the Czech Republic, social pedagogues work within early intervention projects aimed at supporting well-being and self-efficacy with both children and young people and adults. There is no international definition of social pedagogy nor is there a commonly agreed understanding of its relationship with social work, as its interpretation and application have been dependent on the historical, political and cultural aspects of each country. Clearly, it is not therefore possible or desirable to simply lift ideas and practices and place them in another cultural context. It is, however, useful to explore the potential contribution and relationship social pedagogy offers to social work here in the UK. At the time of writing this book, it is probably fair to suggest that social pedagogy in the UK is an eclectic and exciting mix and has been influenced by social pedagogical philosophy, theory and practice from all over the world.

Over the last 10 years, there have been many positive developments within social work organisations and educational institutions embedding and extending the use of social pedagogy into social care practice. At the same time, there has been a growth in knowledge, understanding and academic research of the discipline. ThemPra, a social enterprise providing short courses, qualifications and capacity-building in social pedagogy, and Jacaranda, an organisation providing training and recruitment of social pedagogues have spearheaded these developments. Additionally, the work of Professors Pat Petrie and Claire Cameron, at the Thomas Coram Research Unit at the Institute of Education, have supported the development and application of social pedagogy to social work in the UK.

Before providing an overview of the chapters in this book, it is important to highlight the use of terminology, which we believe is fundamental to approaching social work from a social pedagogical perspective. The term *service user* when referring to individuals who social workers support and work with will be avoided. Instead of this label we will use phrases such as people/individuals we work with/alongside or people/individuals we support. One of the historical key thinkers, the Brazilian educational philosopher and thinker Paulo Freire (1970) (see Chapter 2), wrote extensively in relation to the importance of language and how it can lead to oppressive and discriminatory practice. Language can allow people to be seen as the other and as objects, and in the context of social work and the position of those in receipt of support and services this becomes highly relevant. As we will explore within the book, the ability to recognise and reduce power differentials in our practice is central to achieving social pedagogical goals. Acknowledging the importance of language and power allows us to begin challenging and changing the way power works. We hope that you find this book informative, interesting and inspiring in helping you to develop more creative ways of working as well as being the start of your social pedagogical journey.

Chapter 1

This chapter will explore definitions of social pedagogy and consider how this links to current social work practice and the professional social work standards. The way in which social pedagogy supports and enhances social work practice is discussed throughout the chapter with practice examples.

Chapter 2

This chapter focuses on some of the most influential thinkers, providing a sense of the strong theoretical base of social pedagogical practice, as well as its rich history. It is important to gain an understanding of the historic, social and cultural influences that have shaped social pedagogy whilst also concentrating on its ethical standpoint.

Chapter 3

In this chapter, some of the key theories and concepts used in social pedagogical practice will be discussed. This is not a definitive list and we have chosen to focus on the ones that we feel link to social work practice and provide a good foundation for social pedagogical practice.

Chapter 4

This chapter will focus on the development of social pedagogy within children and family services within the UK. It will provide you with an overview of the areas of social work practice that have embedded social pedagogy within and explore some of the findings from pilot projects funded by the government over the last 10 years.

Chapter 5

In this chapter we will explore the relevance and application of social pedagogy when working alongside adults. It will include an examination of how social pedagogy can support the ideological shift from welfare to well-being, focusing on themes of choice and self-determination. Key pieces of legislation such as the Care Act (2014) are used to demonstrate and discuss how social pedagogy is being expanded into this field of social work.

Chapter 6

In this chapter we concentrate on participation within practice and its significance in demonstrating how social pedagogy aligns with core social work principles of participation, advocacy, empowerment and rights-based work. A number of activities are provided in this chapter to support practical application of the above principles.

Chapter 7

The final chapter refers to risk, risk management and risk competence within social work in relation to children and adults. It will include an exploration of social pedagogical approaches and theories to risk and consider some of the legal, ethical, political and economic factors impacting on practice in this area.

Throughout the chapters we have provided practice examples, research findings and further reading to support your learning and to help you think about how you can begin to use some of the theory, concepts and philosophy in your own direct work, no matter what area of practice you work in.

WHAT IS SOCIAL PEDAGOGY AND HOW DOES IT LINK TO SOCIAL WORK?

LOWIS CHARFE

This first chapter will focus on how we define social pedagogy and social pedagogical practice. It is often difficult for people to give a clear and concise explanation to those who have little knowledge of what it is. Part of the reason for this (to use a good social pedagogical phrase) is that *it depends*. Social pedagogy can be different in different countries and is also influenced by the contexts and situations that it is being used in (Cameron and Moss, 2011b). As Eichsteller and Holthoff (2011a, p. 34) write, social pedagogy is a social construct 'it emerges through dialogue about theory and practice, transcending national boundaries to the extent that inspiring ideas can be influential across different cultures'. In this chapter I will explore the core common values and themes of social pedagogy and try and set out a clear explanation of these theories, practice and inspiring ideas. It is also important to recognise that social pedagogy here in the UK is often seen to be linked to children and their families. This is mainly due to the fact that the majority of the developments have so far been in this area of social work. It is however essential that we recognise that social pedagogical practice can be used across the lifespan and in countries such as Denmark, it is applied to any area of social work and social care 'from birth to 100 years old' (Cameron and Moss, 2011b, p. 7).

This chapter will also consider the historical development of the core theories that have shaped the development of social pedagogy; there will be a more detailed discussion around the key historical thinkers and their influential theories in Chapter 2. It is important that we understand that social pedagogy is not a new idea and has a varied and multilayered history. Hämäläinen (2003, p. 71) points out that social pedagogical practice and theory is older than the concept or use of the term social pedagogy. Here in the UK, social pedagogy can often be seen as the latest fad or trend in social work practice, which has been transported from Europe and in particular from the Scandinavian countries. Stephens (2013, p. 11, cited in Lorenz, 2004) suggests, however, that 'social work tradition in the Anglophone world already contains many of the same elements found in social pedagogy'. Likewise, Eichsteller and Holthoff (2011b) state that social pedagogy uses a wide range of theories from various disciplines and believe it can therefore be transferred and embedded into the way social care practitioners work in the UK.

Defining Social Pedagogy

To understand a theory, concept or idea it is often helpful to look at the words and their meaning as a starting point. Pedagogy is a familiar word to some people in the UK and is often used in the context of formal education. It originates from the Greek word *paidagōgia*, and roughly translates as *to teach* or *to lead a child* and relates to the theory and practice of teaching. In Ancient Greece, there were not only teachers for children of wealthy families but also *family attendants* who were usually slaves (Smith, 2009a). These *paidagogos* (pedagogues) were almost like the equivalent of a modern day nanny in that they cared for and supervised a child outside of school and in every aspect of their daily life. Their role was not only to keep the child safe and look after their health and well-being but also to teach them social skills and manners (Castle, 1961, cited in Smith, 2009a).

The word *social* is one that is used in everyday language here in the UK and can be associated with a wide range of situations, but in essence means related to society (Oxford English Dictionary, 2018). Placing the two words together, social pedagogy broadly refers to the social education of people, but as we deepen our exploration we will consider the wide-ranging philosophical meaning underpinning social pedagogy.

Social pedagogy was first defined in Germany by Karl Mager (1810–1858) and Adolph Diesterweg (1790–1866) around 1850 (Smith, 2009a). At this time in history, Germany was going through great social change, just like in Britain and the majority of European countries. There was a growing recognition of the negative impact that the industrial revolution was having on most of society and many countries, including Germany, had begun to see growing poverty and inequality amongst the working class people (Rothuizen and Harbo, 2017). As industry grew, more people had moved from rural areas to live and work in towns and cities and the living standards and wages had fallen whilst for the wealthiest, theirs had increased. Both Mager and Diesterweg recognised the gap and rising inequality within society as a major problem and one that had not been the intended consequence of industrlisation (Smith, 2009a). Each had a different focus on how to tackle the inequality they saw around them which influenced their different and distinct definitions of social pedagogy. Despite their differences, Mager and Diesterweg were the first people to place the needs of individuals and society alongside the need for education to support people to improve their personal situations (Rothuizen and Harbo, 2017).

Mager defined social pedagogy as the 'theory of all personal, social and moral education in a given society, including the description of what has happened in practice' (translated by Gabriel Thomas, cited in Cameron and Moss, 2011b, p. 8; see also Petrie, 2013, p. 5). In the first part of his definition, Mager is emphasising the point that social pedagogy refers to taking a complete view of the person we are working with. When working with people to support positive change we have to take a holistic approach, which acknowledges not only every part of the person's sense of self, but their connections and the influences of their family, community, the society they live in and their ability to be a *positive* part of that society. The three areas of the *personal*, *social* and *moral* are all equally important and this is what separates social pedagogy from education and social work.

Diesterweg, on the other hand, explained social pedagogy as a framework to guide everyday tasks that could be used in helping people learn the skills they needed to find solutions to the 'social and pedagogical problems that appeared in the modern, emerging industrial society' (Rothuizen and Harbo, 2017, p. 7). Diesterweg linked the idea that to support positive change, people had to be encouraged to transform their own lives using self-development and self-confidence via an education system (Hatton, 2013). Diesterweg's focus was on the micro systems, that of the support system surrounding an individual and their families and certain disadvantaged groups. For him these were the key factors in shaping positive social change. In contrast, Mager was focused on the macro, so the broader social and political systems that impacted or influenced a person's life, and he felt that dealing with inequality and poverty was the responsibility of everybody in society. Here there is a clear link to the sociological debate between structure and agency: the extent to which individuals have free agency to determine their own lives compared to the control exerted by powerful structures and organisations influencing their outcomes (Cunningham and Cunningham, 2014).

Despite their sociological differences, both Diesterweg and Mager agreed that we have to recognise that as individuals, we are social beings with a connection to each other and that social pedagogy can be used to develop a productive and caring society (Rothuizen and Harbo, 2017). This is in stark contrast to the dominant ideology here in modern Britain around the idea of individualisation and personal responsibility. These ideas grew out of the late 1970s with the Conservative government's neoliberal political agenda and with Margaret Thatcher proclaiming in 1987 that 'there's no such thing as society, there are individual men and women and there are families' (Keay, 1987). This ideology began to dominate political thinking, law and policy. Modern social work practice is directed and greatly influenced by political ideology and the policies and ideas of the ruling government (Cunningham and Cunningham, 2014; Ruch et al., 2010). Personal responsibility and promotion of independence has become the main aim of any social work intervention over the last 20 years as a result of the reduction in resources and a growing emphasis towards value for money and target-driven approaches (Trevithick, 2014a). There has been a shift in focus from the importance of the supportive relationship between a service user, their family and the social worker to that of outcomes and target-driven support (Ruch et al., 2010; Trevithick, 2014a). There are now many critics of managerial focused social work, who suggest that the heart has been taken out of social work; one of the most notable in the last few years, being Professor Eileen Munro in her review of the child protection system in 2011. Arguably, the application of Mager and Diesterweg's definitions of social pedagogy can both counter this approach to social work and reclaim and refocus on the importance of the relationship between social workers and the people they support. Human dignity on an individual and societal level, together with well-being, is at the core of social pedagogical practice, in direct contrast to the deficit-based and investigative approach that has become the starting point for social work in the UK (Smith and Whyte, 2008; Trevithick, 2014a). Social pedagogy, therefore, as a philo-sophical, ethical and critical reflective way of working, supports us in placing the relationship right back at the heart of social work practice.

An Educational Approach

Another important focus of social pedagogy is not just that of our emotional connections and relationships with each other, but of the use of education in supporting positive change and development. It is often suggested that social pedagogy is where social work and education meet (Cameron and Moss, 2011b; Petrie, 2013). Hämäläinen (2003, p. 71) states that the devel-opment of social pedagogical practice 'was based on attempts to find educational solutions to social problems'. Social pedagogy should not viewed, however, as an *add on* to social work or a set of methods that can be picked up and used.

 **KEY POINT**

Social pedagogy is not a method, nor even a set of methods. An action is not social pedagogical because certain methods are used therein, but because some methods are chosen and used as a consequence of social pedagogical thought. (Hämäläinen, 2003, p. 77)

So it is not about what is done in practice but how it is done.

It is essential to understand what the term education means in relation to social pedagogy and how this links to social pedagogical practice (Rothuizen and Harbo, 2017). Here in the UK when we use the word education, it is often understood and applied within a very nar-row definition and is related to the formal education that happens in schools and higher educational settings. This definition limits the idea of education and the important role that it plays in supporting people to gain the confidence, skills and the ability to problem solve, to deal with the world around them and make a positive contribution to that world. As Stephens (2013) points out, when we are talking about education with regard to social pedagogy, we are talking about something similar to social learning. To quote Pat Petrie (2011, p. 7), social pedagogy is about:

> … education in the broadest sense of that word … is concerned with the whole child: a physical, thinking, feeling, creative human being in relationship with other people and already contributing to our society.

Remember that even though Petrie (2011) is referring to children, this can be applied equally to adults. By taking this approach it gives us an important focus and allows us to use any situation as an opportunity for growth and development. Any everyday activity can be a chance to help the people we are working with to develop their social, interpersonal life skills, their confidence and promote self-efficacy, so that they are more able to deal with the challenges of life.

KEY POINT

Using an educational approach in social pedagogy is about helping people to develop the skills they need on a personal and social level so that they can be an active and positive member in the world around them.

The idea of using an educational approach is central to social pedagogy and links to modern social work practice in its underpinning ideology. One of the core aims we have as practitioners is that we should not create dependence but support people to live independent lives. As professionals we are led to believe that this should be the main aim of any social work intervention and this can be seen in how it has been embedded into the professional standards relating to social work practice. The *Knowledge and Skills Statement for Child and Family Practitioners* (DfE, 2018a), Section 6, sets out that social workers should be able to:

> Carry out in-depth and ongoing family assessment of social need and risk to children, with particular emphasis on parental capacity and capability to change.

With regard to social workers working with adults, the *Knowledge and Skills Statement* (DoH, 2015b) states:

Social workers should enable people to experience personalised, integrated care and support them to maintain their independence and wellbeing, cope with change, attain the outcomes they want and need, understand and manage risk, and participate in the life of their communities.

(Please note that at the time of writing the *Knowledge and Skills Statement for Social Workers in Adult Services* had been opened up for consultation and the outcome and revised statement had not yet been published.)

The Professional Capability Framework, held by the British Association of Social Workers (2018), also sets out the importance of promoting independence in the Intervention and Skills section of the framework. Here we can see a clear link between social work practice and social pedagogy's broad educational approach (Petrie, 2011). Social pedagogy is about supporting and helping people to develop their own potential to manage their lives and, again to use a social pedagogical phrase, to the point where professionals are no longer needed.

Well-being, Learning and Growth

To bring us up to date, another definition of social pedagogy has been set out by ThemPra (2017b) locating the importance of *well-being, learning* and *growth*. Social pedagogy is based on the humanistic principles and values that 'each person has inherent potential, is valuable, resourceful and can make a meaningful contribution to their wider community, if we find ways to include them' (ThemPra, 2017b). This builds on the work of Karl Mager's definition and links to people including Carl Rogers (1902–1987) and his emphasis on the core conditions needed for effective work with people. The idea of growth is important and again links back to the focus and aim of social work practice as set out in the professional standards mentioned above. Eichsteller and Holthoff (2011a) use the metaphor of the gardener and sculptor to help explain this. So before you go on to read the explanation, let's have a think about the differences between these by having a go at the following exercise.

 **ACTIVITY 1.1**

Gardner and sculptor

Eichsteller and Holthoff (2011a) use this metaphor to explain the focus of social pedagogy in practice.

Write down or discuss with a partner the things that you think a sculptor does, what is their purpose? What kind of tools do they use? How do they shape something?

Now do the same and either write down or discuss what you think a gardener does, what is their main aim? What tools would they use and how do they shape something?

Can you see the differences between what a sculptor and gardener does? How do you think this links to social pedagogy with what you already know about it?

This metaphor is based on the work of John Amos Comenius (1592–1670), a philosopher from the Czech Republic. He challenged the widely held view that children were empty vessels that needed adult teaching to fill them with the knowledge they required (Eichsteller and Holthoff, 2011a). Comenius identified that the main difference between a gardener and a sculptor is that a sculptor will use their tools to shape the material they are using into a form that they desire. A gardener on the other hand will create an environment that allows plants to grow freely and provide the things needed to support them. This is a wonderful metaphor for the core social pedagogical principles of well-being, learning and growth (Eichsteller and Holthoff, 2011b) but also acknowledges the importance of creating environments that encourage and nurture these aspects. This very much links back to Petrie's (2011, p. 7) point around using learning and 'education in its broadest sense' but also to social work practice. In their current research, Andy Bilson, Brie Featherstone and Katie Martin (2017) have identified the impact of poverty and the current government's austerity policies on children and their families involved in the child protection system. There has been an alarming increase in the number of families being investigated under Section 47 of the Children Act (1989) especially with regard to neglect and emotional abuse (Bilson et al., 2017). These assessments investigated the likelihood of a child suffering or likely to suffer significant harm after there have been concerns raised to their local authority about their well-being and safety. The assessment often led to children being placed on the child protection register and families having social work intervention along with contact with other professionals. Many of these families were living in poverty and had been directly affected by changes in welfare policies pushed through under the banner of austerity. Bilson et al. (2017) argue that these families are often living in the most deprived communities in England and that social workers need to have an understanding of the impact of poverty on people's capacity to parent their children. The need to understand how a person's environment and life space impact on them is crucial, as well as understanding how practitioners can support nurturing environments that support children, adults and families to learn and grow (Eichsteller and Holthoff, 2011b).

Social pedagogy makes us recognise the importance of everyday activities no matter how big or small in helping people to grow, learn, develop and increase their sense of well-being. It also recognises that growth is rooted in society and that as human beings we are all connected to the world around us through relationships, families and communities. Growth therefore should happen in two ways: by gaining the skills we need to live independently but also it is fundamental that we can live alongside each other in a positive manner.

This emphasises the need for interdependency and that we are all reliant on other people to help us with this – a clear link to the Relational Universe concept (ThemPra, 2017d) which will be discussed in Chapter 3. These social pedagogical ideas of independence and inter dependence stem from Goethe's (1749–1832) ideas and quote that 'children need two things from their parents: roots and wings' (cited in ThemPra, 2018). It should be argued that the same is also true for adults and that this should be the focus of our work when using social pedagogy.

In being able to support people to learn, grow and feel good about themselves, we need to be able to build positive relationships with the people we are working with. Trevithick (2014b) writes that this is often seen as something that is very easy, but in actual fact takes a lot of skill, practice and reflection; people do not just have great interpersonal skills, they take a lot of working at. The use of relationships is at the centre of any social pedagogical practice (Eichsteller and Holthoff, 2012) and as Bengtsson et al. (2008, p. 9) write, social pedagogy is about 'the conscious use of relationships'. These relationships we form need to be authentic and genuine and based on a firm belief in kindness, 'compassion, open-heartedness and generosity' and 'the sympathetic expansiveness linking self to others' (Stephens, 2013, p. 23). If you think about your favourite school teacher you had as a child they will have often displayed all of the characteristics mentioned above and will have left you with fond memories of them and you will have learnt lots from their teaching. Stephens (2013) goes on to talk about *caritas* and explains that this means going a step further than just being kind and compassionate. It also means that we work in ways and use opportunities that arise to support people to build up their skills, confidence and self-efficacy so that they feel empowered to take control and manage their own lives. As Stephens (2013, p. 27) states, 'Social pedagogues do not want to be in charge'. Practitioners need to have a deeply held respect for human dignity and be able to work in a way that is 'enabling rather than directive' (Stephens, 2013, p. 27). This relational-based practice is carried out within the framework of the Danish concept of the Three Ps (Eichsteller and Holthoff, 2012). This framework, which is discussed in more detail in Chapter 3, sets out the need for us to bring personal parts of our character into the work, complementing the professional self. The positive effects of this approach to practice can be seen in the various pilot projects that have been run here in the UK. As Eichsteller and Holthoff (2012) mention when summarising one of the pilots, it allowed residential workers to feel a more human connection to the children they were caring for within a professional boundary that kept them and the children safe. The children also expressed feelings of being loved and cared for as well as being able to care for each other and having a sense of their own identity. Smith (2009b) in his book *Rethinking Residential Child Care* highlights that many residential workers feel apprehensive about undertaking tasks or working in a way that could be seen as unprofessional. I would suggest that the same applies to social workers due to the professional registration and standards that govern our practice. We are so often told, and rightly so, that we must be professional in all areas of our practice or risk de-registration, with the consequence of not being able to practise as a social worker. However this means that we focus solely on what we see as professional behaviour at the expense of thinking about the importance of our relationships. Here social pedagogy supports and encourages us to work in a more humanistic way and helps develop people's confidence in working in more creative ways that bring fulfilment and enjoyment back into their practice. When running training events with practitioners we often ask people what brought them into the profession and the answer is nearly always lead by the heart: people wanted to help make a change in people's lives. And as Smith (2009b) and many others point out, social pedagogy allows us to use relationship-based, positive practice where both the practitioner and person they are working with will grow and learn together.

Empowerment

Returning to empowerment, which was mentioned previously, it is key that we recognise that we do not give people empowerment. I often hear students I visit on social work placements talk about how they have empowered the service user they are working with in the course of their work. Empowerment, however, is not ours to give; as Eichsteller and Holthoff (2012) state, empowerment is about human rights and people having agency or control over the decisions that are made in their lives. Social pedagogical relationships focus on the need for equality and equal respect for each other and to make sure that 'power is used not as a form of control but as a responsibility' (Eichsteller and Holthoff, 2012, p. 44). This clearly links to the key ideas of anti-oppressive practice, a term all social work students and practitioners are aware of and strive to achieve in their work. Bandura (1997) very clearly points out that positive change comes from a person being supported to find the skills and ability within themselves to make the changes they would like to see in their own lives, and he called this self-efficacy. This also means that people are then better prepared and able to transfer these skills to other situations that arise in the future and can deal with them in a more positive way. Social pedagogy and concepts such as the Diamond Model discussed in Chapter 3 (Eichsteller and Holthoff, 2011a) reflect this important point by placing empowerment directly across from relationships. This reminds us that positive relationships are important but that empowerment is separate from these but directly linked. It also encourages us to be mindful about our *role* when working with people. All social pedagogical relationships and work need to be purposeful, with the ultimate aim in supporting growth, development and well-being. Storø (2013) writes that there must be a reason for all of the work that a social pedagogue does even if this is not clearly understood by the person they are working with due maybe to their age or cognitive capacity. This brings me back to the second important point Mager (1844, cited in Cameron and Moss, 2011b) set out in defining social pedagogy and that is its direct link to our work with people. In Thomas's translation of Mager's famous definition, he sets out that social pedagogy is also the 'description of what has happened in practice' (translated by Gabriel Thomas, cited in Cameron and Moss, 2011b, p. 8; see also

Petrie, 2013, p. 5). This important point links social pedagogical theory to its direct application to practice; it is an applied theory that requires us to reflect on what is happening as well as setting out a framework recognising the impact of the personal, social and moral parts of a person's life.

Social Justice

The final point to make about social pedagogy links to Mager and Diesterweg's shared agreement that society and not just individuals are equally important. I have focused on relationship-based practice but social pedagogy also makes us focus on the link between individuals and society. Promotion of equality and social justice is at the heart of all social pedagogical practice. There is recognition that working with individuals and groups is important, but if there is to be real change then equality and social justice on a societal level need to be achieved. 'The goal of social pedagogy is, firstly, to improve the unequal social conditions by socio-political means, and secondly to enable individuals to fight their own battle to improve social conditions' (Sunker and Braches-Chyrek, 2009, cited in Stephens, 2013, p. 68). Once again we can make a link to a sociological theory that is helpful in supporting practitioners to do this. C. Wright Mills's (1959, cited in Cunningham and Cunningham, 2014) idea of *sociological imagination* asks us to think about the broader social structures that affect and impact on people's lives. He talked about the need to not only see the individual and their 'problem' but to understand the 'social, economic and historical circumstances' that the person was subjected to (Wright Mills, 1959, cited in Cunningham and Cunningham, 2014, p. 3). To help us gain a better understanding of what he meant by this, complete the following exercise.

ACTIVITY 1.2

Structure/agency debate

The debate about which has more influence and control over our lives is an ongoing debate amongst sociologists, but what do you think?

Think of a recent decision you made in your life, this could be as simple as making a drink or as big as deciding to change jobs. Think about whether you made this decision based on your own free will. For instance, if you look at making a drink, you might want to think about if you were feeling thirsty, what did you fancy to drink? Were you out on a walk or at work? Was this decision linked to your health?

Now thinking about this decision, make a list of all of the organisations or structures that have maybe had an influence on how you made it. Think broadly around this and consider things close to you, such as your family, and things that may seem to be on a global level, such as any international organisations or laws. So going back to the example of making a drink, you might think about things such as the environment. Were you at work? Was there an expectation that you make each other drinks? Has advertising had an influence on what you choose to drink? Are there cultural influences such as the British love of tea?

Reflecting back on this activity, what do you think now about the structure/agency debate? Which if any has more impact on your life do you think?

By taking this standpoint and being able to have a wider understanding of the social context of a person's life, means that as practitioners we are able to work in an anti-oppressive, anti-discriminatory way. We see the person we are working with as an individual but also recognise that there are things beyond their control and how these have impacted on their ability to make the changes they might want or need. For example, you may be working with a person who is living in an unclean house, yet this is a privately rented property that is not maintained by their landlord. Due to a lack of affordable social housing in their area and a housing benefit cap, they are unable to move or may not want to move as their entire social and support network such as their friends, family, job, children's schools, etc. are in that area. In this situation it is unhelpful to continually comment on and assess them on the standard of their house every time you visit them without recognising the factors that are beyond their control but that have a direct impact on their lives.

By using a sociological imagination, this places a requirement on us as professionals and fellow human beings to challenge and change unfair social structures as well as reminding us how important it is to keep looking at how problems are constructed at a societal level. When I worked with care leavers as a social worker, I supported many of them to make claims for welfare benefits. Due to government regulations, some of them had to have what was known as an *estrangement interview* where they would be called into the local benefits office and interviewed by the person assessing their benefit claim. The purpose of this interview was to check that the young person was entitled to benefits but also that they were not receiving financial help from their parents or direct family members. Part of the interview entailed being asked to give very personal details and accounts about why they had been taken into care and how much contact and support they received from their parents. As you can imagine, this was incredibly difficult for the majority of the young people and they found the questions intrusive and very upsetting. I worked with the Head of the Assessment Unit at our local benefit office and we formed a working agreement that any young person who made an application for benefits would have a supporting statement from their social worker. This would be proof enough for the assessment team and the *estrangement interview* would not be needed.

Hopefully this gives you a clear example of how we can promote social justice on a relatively small scale and within a structure, like our benefits system, that is often seen as rigid. Finding the loopholes and being able to think outside the box and continuing to try and change unjust systems is crucial when promoting social justice. As I write this chapter we have just celebrated the 100 year anniversary of the Representation of the People Act (1918), which after years of struggle by the Suffragettes and working class movements, saw all working class men and *some* women being able to vote in elections. This just goes to show how powerful individuals can be when they come together to challenge systems that oppress sections of our society.

Conclusion

In this chapter we have explored how social pedagogy is a philosophical and ethical way of working based on deep respect for people and is not a method. We should use social pedagogy as a lens to view the world around us, which then in turn informs the way we work with people. The importance of *Haltung* (your value base), discussed in more detail in Chapter 3, and this ethical focus mean that social pedagogy is part of your whole being; therefore in our practice we are not 'just a pair of hands' or 'the professional' (Eichsteller, 2010, p. 4). It also encourages us to acknowledge that the people we are working with have value and are equal human beings and that our relationships with them have to be based on equality, inclusion and true participation. It supports us to work in a more creative way where we can challenge the systems-led focus of modern social work. It is not a magic wand and social pedagogy will often place us at odds with process, colleagues and other professionals, but social work *is* complex and difficult and *should* be, as we are dealing with people and their lives. People deserve social workers who value them as human beings and will face the challenge to advocate, support and fight for their rights and put all of their head, heart and hands into supporting their well-being, learning and growth.

Further Reading

Professional Capabilities Framework for Social Work in England:
www.basw.co.uk/system/files/resources/Detailed%20level%20descriptors%20for%20all%20
    domains%20wi%20digital%20aug8.pdf
www.thempra.org.uk/social-pedagogy/
www.thempra.org.uk/social-pedagogy/key-concepts-in-social-pedagogy/thempras-social-
    pedagogy-tree/

SOCIAL PEDAGOGICAL KEY THINKERS

LOWIS CHARFE

In this chapter, I will explore a number of influential individuals along an historical timeline. This will provide an understanding of both the social and historical developments and their contribution to the development of social pedagogy. Many of the key figures explored here are progressive educational thinkers, some of whom were seen as part of the New Education Movement that swept across Europe in the 1800s. This was an important movement as it challenged widely held beliefs around education, where lessons were taught in rote style and children were expected to learn by repeating what was being taught to them. This movement also fought for children to be seen as an equal to adults, as competent human beings, promoted children's rights and pushed social pedagogical thinking into mainstream education and broader society. We saw in Chapter 1 that the 'personal, social and moral education' (Cameron and Moss, 2011b, p. 8; see also Petrie, 2013) should be the key focus of social pedagogical practice. Therefore it is no surprise that educational philosophers are heavily represented and are one of the key strands of social science theory that underpin social pedagogical practice (see ThemPra's social pedagogy tree, on their website, www.thempra.org.uk/social-pedagogy/key-concepts-in-social-pedagogy/thempras-social-pedagogy-tree/)

It is crucial that we understand the societal context within which each historical thinker was living and as we explore each one, it will be useful for you to consider this. Some of their ideas or practices may seem to be just common sense and widely accepted in modern society, or they might be seen as extreme in nature and would be socially unacceptable now. For example, Jean-Jacques Rousseau (1712–1778), the French social philosopher, developed the idea that nature was the most important influencing factor on a child's development and that adults should provide the right environment to support this (a key social pedagogical concept). He is credited with developing the concept of child-centred learning and yet he sent all five of his children to *foundling* hospitals, which are in modern terms, orphanages (Doyle and Smith, 2007; Eichsteller et al., 2014). If we think about congruence then his actions could be seen at odds with his ideas; however it is important that we understand them in relation to the moral values of the society he lived in at that time. Rousseau defended his action by stating that he would not have been able to support them and it is now widely accepted that due to his personal character, he did not possess the skills required to be an adequate parent (Doyle and Smith, 2007).

As we move through the last 300 years, one final fact that needs to be acknowledged is that the majority of these key thinkers were white, often wealthy males who were in privileged social positions, able to influence, challenge and change social structures and thinking. These factors are worth noting when considering people such as Maria Montessori, as it helps us remember the incredible struggle they undertook to have their ideas recognised and applied to practice. Also it is important that we recognise those that used their social positions to challenge prejudicial ideas and discriminatory practices. They also struggled to change the societal norms and challenge powerful structures such as religion, monarchies and governments. Hopefully their struggles inspire us to see that nothing is set in stone and cannot be changed within the world around us. As Margaret Mead (1901–1978), the cultural anthropologist, famously said: 'Never doubt that a small group of thoughtful, committed citizens can change the world; indeed, it's the only thing that ever has.'

Pestalozzi (1746–1827)

Johann Heinrich Pestalozzi was born in Switzerland and is viewed as one of the most important, influential key thinkers and credited with developing a holistic approach to education using *head, heart and hands* (Eichsteller et al., 2014). Pestalozzi built on the ideas of Rousseau and the notion that children are not empty vessels needing adults to fill them with knowledge, but have a great capacity for learning (Smith, 2009c). Unlike Rousseau, Pestalozzi managed to put his ideas into practice and developed teaching methods based on his ideas around 'cultivating the children's own powers of seeing, judging and reasoning and encouraging their self-activity and spontaneity' (Eichsteller et al., 2014, p. 34). Returning to the metaphor of the tree, he believed that each child was like a seed and had the potential to grow and develop if the conditions were right (Smith, 2009c). Like other key thinkers, Pestalozzi was also interested in how to promote equality, and social justice was at the heart of his thinking (Hämäläinen, 2003; Hatton, 2013). He firmly believed that education was the way to solve social issues. Through his own life experiences he recognised the importance of loving relationships and the need to help people improve their own social conditions. His mother and a maid raised Pestalozzi after the death of his father, so he had experienced first hand what it was like to live in a household that had a limited income. He understood and tried to address the tension between the individual and their needs with that of society (Smith, 2009c). At first he saw this through the lens of political movements, but after the death of a close friend he began to see the importance of education in addressing this tension and supporting positive social change (Eichsteller et al., 2014; Smith, 2009c).

One of his key ideas was that of *Anschauung* and the use of direct observation (Eichsteller et al., 2014; Smith, 2009c). Pestalozzi believed that in order to support a child to grow, learn and develop we have to understand how that child comprehends and interacts with the world around them. To do this we have to use reflection and direct observation, termed by Pestalozzi as *Anschauung*. The social pedagogue would observe a child and then would use their understanding of that child's abilities and character to help create an environment that encourages self-efficacy. *Anschauung* would not be used to then try and shape a child into what the social pedagogue thinks they should be.

Due to his belief in nature and the natural laws of the world, Pestalozzi understood the need for a holistic approach to education and to develop a 'child's heart, mind and body in harmonious unity' (Eichsteller et al., 2014, p. 34). The balance of all three is important and led to the key social pedagogical concept of *Head, Heart and Hands*. (This will be discussed in more detail in Chapter 3.) In all social pedagogical practice there must be equal weight given to each aspect for there to be positive and balanced practice. Pestalozzi highlighted the problems of just focusing on one area at the detriment of the others (Smith, 2009c). With regard to the *head*, Pestalozzi recognised the need to step away from the traditional rote teaching methods where children were taught to recite information they needed (just think about how you learnt your times tables or the alphabet). Instead he believed that children did not just need to know the answers to questions but rather they needed to develop the ability to work them out themselves (Eichsteller et al., 2014). This was a fundamental change in the teaching of children at this point in history, as often children were seen as mini adults and lacking in the ability for free thought and actions. So helping children become curious and use their imagination was at the centre of Pestalozzi's ideas and by using *Anschauung* a pedagogue could engage any child by using things that they found interesting and made them curious to learn.

With regard to the *heart*, Pestalozzi believed that this was equally important and his teachings were based on his Christian beliefs and values. The moral education of children was a vital part of their education and development and this had to be done with love, as Pestalozzi stated:

> ... the elevation of ourselves to a sense of the inner dignity of our nature, and of the pure, higher, godly being, which lies within us. This sense is not developed by the power of our mind in thought, but is developed by the power of our heart in love. (Eichsteller et al., 2014, p. 35)

Pestalozzi's translated this into practice and understood that physical punishment served no purpose in helping to support learning and so he banned physical punishments such as flogging in his schools. A brave and unusual step at this time in history and one that was met with astonishment by many in society (Smith, 2009c). But this also recognised the importance of the relationship between the teacher and a child and the impact this had on a child's ability to learn and develop. For Pestalozzi, if a child was not shown love, empathy and kindness then 'neither the physical not the intellectual powers [would] develop naturally' (Eichsteller et al., 2014, p. 35). So the heart played a fundamental part in learning.

The *hand* element for Pestalozzi related to the significance of the physical aspects of learning. He believed that activities were key to helping children learn and that education should not just focus on intelligence and knowledge (Smith, 2009c). Everyday activities and situations could be seen as an opportunity to learn and Pestalozzi identified this in his own experiences of his childhood. Within the schools he set up he had wanted children to learn skills such as spinning and weaving (Eichsteller et al., 2014) so that they could be self-reliant. Again focusing on the need for the practical application of education and teaching.

Pestalozzi's ideas are still central to social pedagogical practice, through the concept of balancing the three areas of head, heart and hands to the focus on loving relationships. His idea of *Anschauung* and its link to life world orientation mean that when we take this philosophical way of working we are able to work in a truly person-centred way. He also identified the need for social justice: 'in Aristotle's terms he would put that which is "right" or good before that which is "correct"' (Smith, 2009c) – another key point that we should all value and use to guide our own social pedagogical practice.

Grundtvig (1783–1872)

Nikolai Frederick Grundtvig was born in Denmark and is one of the key Danish historical thinkers. He was a prolific writer and wrote many essays on Danish life at that time which focused on politics, history, theology (religious traditions and beliefs) and education, amongst other topics (Smith, 2011). Grundtvig's father was a Lutheran pastor and as a religious man, like Pestalozzi, Grundtvig's religious beliefs underpinned his work. After finishing his studies at the University of Copenhagen, he became a tutor until his father, due to ill health, asked him to take over his pastoral duties, something he was reluctant to do at that time (Smith, 2011). Grundtvig's ideas meant that he ran into trouble on many occasions after producing articles that were in opposition to the main teachings of the church. This meant that Grundtvig spent long periods banned from preaching sermons and this cemented his belief in religion being led by the *common* people and not by religious figures. He challenged what 'he perceived to be the oppressive dogma in theology, politics and pedagogy' (Hatton, 2013, p. 28). Like Pestalozzi, he believed that people had the capacity for self-efficacy and had the resources within themselves to change their own lives for the better and did need to look to a higher power such as God to achieve this. This was seen as a very contentious and radical point of view, but Grundtvig believed that when people understood and became aware of the oppressive social structures that impacted on their lives, then they would be able to challenge and change these. It is worth noting that in Grundtvig's lifetime, massive social changes were happening throughout Europe. In 1848 across Europe *people's revolutions* began to happen, starting in Sicily and spreading to countries as far as France (Harman, 2008). 1848 is often noted as being the *Year of Revolution* as working class people across Europe began to challenge the old order and fought to remove the power and structures of monarchies that had kept them oppressed and poor (Harman, 2008). At this time, scholars such as Karl Marx and Fredrick Engels were writing and publishing key ideas around communism, socialism and the transferring of power from rich monarchs and governments to ordinary people. In Denmark after the *Year of Revolution* there were lasting reforms that removed the power of the monarchy with the setting up of the Constitutional Assembly in October 1848. This could be seen as the foundation stone of the Danish constitution and helps explain why Denmark is seen as one of the most liberal and equal countries in the world (Lawson, 1994).

With regard to social pedagogy, Grundtvig developed Folk High Schools after visiting Robert Owen here in the UK and seeing the work he was undertaking with regard to educational reform. Grundtvig's idea of Folk High Schools was that these would be a place where people could learn practical skills whilst encouraging people to become empowered to make change in the community and society around them. All teaching was to be based on 'life, insight and practical ability' (Grundtvig, 1832, cited in Lawson, 1994, p. 614) and offered people the chance to gain enlightenment through student-led education. An important feature of these schools was the idea of the *fellowship* between students and teachers. This meant that there was true participation between students and teachers in shared teaching, learning and the running of these schools. Grundtvig explained that this approach was based on humanistic ideas and the understanding of the living word:

> I saw life, real human life, as it is lived in this world, and saw at once that to be enlightened, to live a useful and enjoyable human life, most people did not need books at all, but only a genuinely kind heart, sound common sense, a kind good ear, a kind good mouth, and then liveliness to talk with really enlightened people, who would be able to arouse their interest and show them how human life appears when the light shines upon it. (1856, quoted in Borish, 1991, p. 18, cited by Smith, 2011)

The importance of seeing the world from other people's perspectives was important as well as being able to live in communities where everybody was valued and accepted no matter their differences. This ideology has proved instrumental in Danish civil society over the last 60 or 70 years and Grundtvig's influence has been said to have helped fight the rise of fascism that swept across many European countries throughout the 20th century (Lawson, 1994; Smith, 2011). He also reminds us of the value of human potential and the importance that relationships play in helping this to develop, which is at the heart of all social pedagogical practice. A clear link can be made to social work/care practice too.

Natorp (1854–1924)

Paul Natorp was born in Germany and, like Mager, Diesterweg and others, was extremely aware of the effects of industrialisation on the society around him. It is widely recognised that he was the first person to develop social pedagogical practice, which came about from his work around educational reform (Eichsteller et al., 2014; Smith, 2009a). Because of this, he is seen as the birth father of social pedagogy (Eichsteller et al., 2014) and one of the most significant of all social pedagogy historical thinkers. Natorp became a social philosopher and professor at the University of Marburg after finishing his own studies and along with his colleagues established social pedagogical thinking as an academic discipline. This was important as it moved social pedagogy from being a set of ideas and concepts that other social philosophers such as Mager and Diesterweg had written about, into a subject that was researched and taught within a university setting. This gave social pedagogy a new standing within education and in turn supported its application into practice.

Due to the ongoing debates around the impact of industrialisation on individuals, community and society, Natorp believed that the community was the most important factor in this equation. He was greatly influenced by the work of Plato and his ideas around the connection between individuals and the state (Eichsteller et al., 2014; Hämäläinen, 2003). For Plato and in turn Natorp, individuals formed the *just state*, which set out the rules by which people lived alongside each other in harmony. Everybody, no matter their class, understood their roles and duties and what was expected of them with regard to their obligation to the community, thus linking everyone together (Wright, 2012). Plato saw the education of children and adults playing an important part of the *just state* as it helped people to understand their roles and obligations (Wright, 2012). Natorp was also influenced by the ideas of Kant, a German philosopher who developed the idea of respecting and treating people fairly, 'seeing them as subjects in their own rights instead of treating them as means to an end' (Eichsteller et al., 2014, p. 38). This key concept can be seen in modern social work as anti-oppressive and anti-discriminatory practice. Kant fundamentally believed in the potential and value of each human being and that 'We should not merely treat others with respect out of fear of a higher power, but because this is reasonable if we want to be treated with dignity ourselves', a philosophic idea that became known as the *moral imperative* (Eichsteller et al., 2014, p. 38). This key idea can be seen as the foundation for all social pedagogical practice and is at the heart of the Diamond Model developed by Eichsteller and Holthoff (2011a).

For there to be positive change and a harmonious society, Natorp believed that there needed to be a focus on supporting communities, education and reducing the gap between rich and poor. He pictured this taking place in three social spaces: first the household (which sits within a community), then in schools (which also sit within a community) and finally in free adult education (Smith, 2009a). For Natorp all education, no matter where it happened in any of these three identified social spaces, was social education or to use the German term, *Sozialpädagogik* (Eichsteller et al., 2014). This idea was also greatly influenced by the work of Pestalozzi and the ideas he published in his novel *Lienhard and Gertrud* which addressed and gave directions on how to challenge social inequality (Eichsteller et al., 2014; Smith, 2009a). Natorp spelt out the link between education and social change as:

... all pedagogy should be social, that is, that in the philosophy of education the interaction of educational processes and society must be taken into consideration. (Natorp, 1899, 1907, 1920, cited in Hämäläinen, 2003, p. 73)

This was a different perspective from the welfare-led approach that was influential in Germany at that time (Hämäläinen, 2003). Natorp argued that there was a lack of social cohesion in Germany and that the issue was not one of poverty and a lack of material objects. To see it as such lays the blame at the feet of working class people who were already oppressed by a capitalist system. He also went against the accepted doctrine of the church, who for hundreds of years before had set out the moral framework for acceptable behaviour and was seen as the only place that people could receive salvation for misdemeanours and immoral behaviour. Natorp dismissed this ideology and believed that we are all responsible for shaping the world around us instead of leaving this to some higher power, a radical stance to take at that time in history (Eichsteller et al., 2014). For him, the important point was to understand the link between the individual and society and vice versa, but unlike the sociological debates between structure and agency, he understood that both sides of the issue needed to be addressed. Social justice, therefore, is as important as the individual and whilst 'a theoretic understanding of the problem is important, it has to be complemented by practical action' (Eichsteller et al., 2014, p. 39). Throughout his life, Natorp tried to develop educational opportunities for people often excluded from mainstream education at that time, such as the working class. He also combined the person-centred and community-centred aspects of education in his concept of social pedagogy (Eichsteller et al., 2014). This link between the two is still at the core of current social pedagogical practice and Natorp's theories are as relevant today as they were in his lifetime when set against the current backdrop of neoliberalism and austerity agendas of many governments across Europe.

Montessori (1870–1952)

Maria Montessori was born in Italy to a family who recognised the importance of education. Her mother was well educated and an enthusiastic reader and valued her daughter's education, which was unusual at that time (American Montessori Society, 2018). It is worth bearing in mind the position of women in European countries at this point in history: there were very clear gender divides within societies and in particularly with regard to education. Around the same time, Karl and Jenny Marx were seen as dangerous radicals for ensuring their three surviving daughters were well educated as well as dismissing religion and refusing to send them to church (Holmes, 2014). Maria was encouraged and supported by her mother and flew in the face of convention at an early age by studying at an all-boys technical institute as she had hopes of becoming an engineer (American Montessori Society, 2018). Her career path, however, took a change of direction and after persevering she was finally accepted into the University of Rome. She went on to become one of the first women in Italy to graduate from medical school as a physician, which was no mean feat for a woman of the time (American Montessori Society, 2018; Eichsteller et al., 2014).

It was through her work on the university's psychiatric wards and her keen interest in education, that she began to develop her educational approaches. Many of the children she cared for were deemed to be severely disabled and unable to be educated (American Montessori Society, 2018; Eichsteller et al., 2014) and she recognised the need for children to receive care as well as education. Like many other key thinkers Montessori was greatly influenced by the work of Rousseau and began to develop teaching methods using his ideas as a base. Like him, Montessori believed that nature was an important factor and that education needed to take a holistic approach to a child. She began by creating teaching methods that firstly helped children develop their senses. As she wrote:

> It is essential to let nature have its own way as far as possible; the more freedom children are allowed to develop, the quicker and more perfectly they will attain higher forms and functions. (Montessori, cited in Eichsteller et al., 2014, p. 40; see also Röhrs, 1994)

Montessori saw the capacity in children to learn and her early work focused on very young children. Her approach was truly child-centred and she understood that children were not small versions of adults, but unique individuals that had the ability to lead their own learning. She was aware that young children were like sponges and had the ability to absorb information and learn about the world around them (Eichsteller et al., 2014; Röhrs, 1994). For Montessori, therefore, the correct environment was a key factor in supporting children to learn and ultimately direct their own learning and fulfil their potential. Her belief in children's rights extended into her practice and she would encourage children to design the classrooms as well as develop the rules and expected codes of behaviour, with the idea of helping a child develop their own moral autonomy. Children were encouraged to understand and determine what was right and wrong behaviour and not just follow given rules. Being able to determine these meant that children were able to gain a deeper understanding as they linked these to their own selves and their lives. For Montessori having freedom was an important factor but she also recognised that children needed to learn to acquire this alongside having responsibilities. This was a key relationship and she believed that one did not exist without the other, and by using activities which assisted children to develop both, they were able to develop self-discipline, self-efficacy and a *Haltung* (value base) as well as gaining practical skills and knowledge (Röhrs, 1994). In the promotion of freedom and self-discipline, her teaching sessions involved activities that encouraged the development of all five senses, coordination and movement of the body, fine and gross motor skills and the building of skills acquisition (Eichsteller et al., 2014). Each of these skills was repeated daily until a child had mastered them; and then once mastered the ability for the child to see their progress was vitally important.

But one of the most important elements of Montessori's work is her link between theory and practice and her desire to develop scientific educational theories. This evolved from a profound understanding of the importance of observation in helping to comprehend the nature and ability of a child, observing growth and development and seeing each child's potential. Eichsteller and Holthoff's (2011b) analogy of being the gardener in social pedagogy stems from Montessori's educational theories around the link between environment and learning and growth. Being able to observe somebody in their own environment means that you gain a better understanding of their capabilities and can support them to work on areas of weakness by adapting the environment or tasks to encourage and assist with this. Montessori did not just talk about the need for observation and reflection but actually practised this herself when developing her theories and writing teaching plans. She would try out tasks and activities and then adjust these accordingly to her reflections and observations. She also insisted on the need for teachers to be trained and that they should see themselves as instruments in the scientific environment of educating children:

> Instead of talking he must learn to be silent; instead of instructing he must observe; instead of presenting the proud dignity of one who desires to appear infallible he must don the robe of humility. (Montessori, 1976, p. 123, cited in Röhrs, 1994, p. 177)

Even though she advanced educational theories and more importantly teaching practice, there have been many critics of her work, who have said that she paid little attention to the cognitive or biological capacity or social factors influencing a child's ability (Röhrs, 1994). Her observations were criticised for being subjective as she ignored, or would fail to fully question or analyse, outcomes that did not fit her theory. This led to some believing that her work was often at times vague and ambiguous (Eichsteller et al., 2014; Röhrs, 1994). However, there is no doubt that Montessori has been hugely influential within the field of education and social pedagogy. Her theories, even though some may argue that they lack academic rigour, give us a framework or philosophy by which to lead our lives and professional practice.

Nohl (1879–1960)

At this point in the historical development of social pedagogy it is worth mentioning Herman Nohl, the German philosopher and educationalist, and his work around the theory of hermeneutics. Hermeneutics tasks us with being able to see and understand a person's life from their perspective. Once we are able to do this by observing and comprehending their interactions with the world around them, we can then establish ways to support them to make positive changes. Hermeneutic theory has had a dominant position in the German tradition of social pedagogy ever since (Hämäläinen, 2003, p. 70).

   After the use of collective education by the Nazi Party in controlling German society and developing a totalitarian state, social pedagogy 'became more critical, revealing a critical attitude towards society and taking the structural factors of society that produce social suffering into consideration' (Hämäläinen, 2003, p. 71). At this point social pedagogy was to become more aligned with social work practice, creating a theoretical framework for professional social work on the basis of the work of Nohl around hermeneutic philosophy.

Korczak (1878–1942)

Janusz Korczak was born in Warsaw, Poland, to wealthy Jewish parents and is credited as an influential thinker not because he developed theories but because of his actions. Like Maria Montessori, Korczak fundamentally believed in the capacity of children and their rights to have equity within society. He had grown up being aware of the injustices and inequality within Polish society and this influenced his *Haltung* and beliefs in the importance of challenging inequality at all levels and in all areas of life. He strove to shape a world that was fairer for all, but foremost for children, who he felt were often ignored.

His passion and warmth undoubtedly helped him in his medical career as a doctor in a Jewish children's hospital and he was said to have been an excellent and compassionate one (Eichsteller et al., 2014). He began to realise that using medicine could only solve the physical symptoms of an illness and that it was also important to solve the social issues that led to and impacted on people's health (Lewowicki, 1997). Again Korczak fully understood the significant link between individuals and society, which is at the core of social pedagogy. He was another influential key thinker that was inspired by the teachings of Pestalozzi and people within the New Education Movement such as Montessori (Lewowicki, 1997). But he had a wide range of interest not just in regard to education and medicine and read the works of people such as Tolstoy, which deepened his belief in social justice and socialism (Lewowicki, 1997). It was this moral stance (*Haltung*) that directed his approach when he took over the running of a residential children's home for Jewish orphans. His strong *Haltung* influenced every aspect of the running of the home (Eichsteller, 2017) and it was of utmost importance to Korczak that all the children living there were seen as equals, that this really was their home where there was a shared responsibility and care and love was given to everybody, child and adult alike (Eichsteller et al., 2014; Lewowicki, 1997). Within the home, children set up a parliament to help create rules and assist in decision-making, a newspaper to share ideas and thoughts and a court to deal with disputes (Eichsteller, 2017; Eichsteller et al., 2014).

His time with the children helped Korczak shape his ideas and practices and he developed a children's charter known as Magna Charta Libertatis which he published in 1919 (Eichsteller, 2017; Lewowicki, 1997). This set out the fundamental rights Korczak believed children should have but also the right to protection from overprotective adults and their aims and beliefs of what was right for a child (Eichsteller, 2017). To this end he created three key points for the charter:

1   The right of the child to die.
2   The right of the child to live for today.
3   The right of the child to be what she or he is.

(Eichsteller, 2017)

The first point is often seen as quite abhorrent and people find it difficult to agree with or even consider the fact that children have the right to die. As adults we often see our role, whether personally or professionally, as making sure children are safeguarded, protected and cared for and this is in direct conflict with Korczak's first key principle. But here he is asking us to consider whether we are being overprotective and potentially stifling the child's growth out of our own concern for their safety. We only need to think about how many children in modern Britain do not play outside their homes with their friends within their own neighbourhoods, out of sight of their parents or carers. How many children often walk to school unaccompanied by an adult? Korczak would say that this is removing a child's opportunity to learn about the world around them and 'disregards the right to freedom, self-expression and self-determination' (Eichsteller, 2017, p. 379). However, a child's safety was of the upmost concern to Korczak and he would not have allowed the free will of a child to come before their safety if they were at risk of death or serious harm. Each child he cared for would have different boundaries depending on their understanding and ability to manage perceived harmful situations. In all other instances he believed that if adults could allow themselves to accept that every child has the right to die, then we allow every child the opportunity in life, to truly be in charge of their own lives and care for them in a meaningful participatory way.

Like Montessori, Korczak believed that observation and communication with children were the most significant tools an adult could employ in helping them to understand, support and care for a child as well as to safeguard them. When implementing a change or a new approach, he would observe, reflect and then adjust his practice and as such never did something because it seemed to be the right thing to do, but rather because it would have a long-lasting impact and support true participation of all the children he was caring for.

In Korczak, we have a powerful example of the importance of living every aspect of your life by the guiding principles of your *Haltung*. Equity between the children, his staff and himself was that important to him that it is well documented that Korczak's life ended alongside the children in his care in the gas chambers of the infamous Treblinka extermination camp. Even when given the opportunity to spare his own life he refused. He also encourages us to see children as equals and to practise in a child-led and participatory way in every aspect of our lives. With regard to the social construction of childhood, he has helped challenge and given clear practical examples of the ability of children to determine their own lives and navigate the world around them; as one of my favourite Korczak quotes states: 'there are no more fools amongst children than amongst adults' (Korczak, 2007, cited in Eichsteller, 2017, p. 391).

Vygotsky (1896–1934)

Vygotsky may well be a name that many of you are aware of and as a Russian psychologist his name and work is widely recognised. He was fascinated by and focused on human development and the impact of biology and social factors on a person's ability to develop new skills and knowledge. With regard to social pedagogical practice his Zone of Proximal Development (ZPD) theory is key in being able to understand how we support a person to reach their identified aims (Eichsteller et al., 2014). This concept will be explored in more depth in Chapter 3.

Like many of the other influential thinkers, he recognised that children and adults have hidden potential and his work challenges us to see this too. It also asks that we reflect on our practice and make sure that instead of doing things for people, we are allowing them to learn for themselves. One of the most important elements of this theory was that he also encouraged learning amongst peers. Vygotsky identified how a skilled peer can often be more important to a child's learning in comparison to that directed by a teacher. This is because a child learns much more through imitating and interacting with the world around them than being made to sit and listen to somebody who is deemed to be more able (Hatton, 2013).

Another key feature of Vygotsky's work is the importance of creativity and imagination, which he believed were at the core of growth and development and without them we would just keep recreating old ideas (Vygotsky, 2004). If we can engage in creative thinking then we are able to challenge the 'structural and class oppression' we face in modern society (Hatton, 2013, p. 31). Here in the UK we can see some wonderful examples of creativity being used to shape and develop practice as well as challenge oppressive structures. One of the most recent was a research project called *Getting Things Changed* (Williams, 2018a), which looked at how much participation adults with learning disabilities had in decisions made about their lives and how this can be meaningfully increased. The use of arts and music was at the centre of this co-produced research and it found that by using creative methods people with a learning disability take control over decisions in their own lives and challenge the way they are perceived by society (Williams, 2018b). This also links to the work around arts and creativity completed by Helen Chambers and Pat Petrie (2009) and their development of the *Learning Framework for Artist Pedagogues* – again highlighting the important role that creativity has in supporting transformation with groups that are seen as disadvantaged and social excluded.

Freire (1921–1997)

Our final social pedagogical historical thinker is Brazilian-born Paulo Freire, who was a qualified lawyer, educational thinker and philosopher. Even though he was born into what would be considered a middle class family, his childhood was greatly impacted by the Great Depression in the 1930s (Eichsteller et al., 2014; Shaull, cited in Freire, 1996). This financial crisis started in 1929 in America and by the early 1930s had impacted on the lives of people living in Brazil and around the world (Shaull, cited in Freire, 1996). As Freire (1996, p. 12) famously wrote, this forced his family into poverty and to live alongside the 'wretched of the earth'. He experienced hunger and fell behind at school and clearly remembered how difficult it was to concentrate on his education and the impact poverty and hunger had on his ability to learn. At the age of 11, Freire decided that he would 'dedicate his life to the struggle against hunger' (Shaull, 1996, cited in Freire, 1996, p. 12) and this early experience was a turning point as he began to realise the link between politics, economics, society and poverty in the oppression of the poor. It was this social injustice and the role paternalistic systems such as the education system played in this oppression that made Freire develop an educational approach that directly challenged and supported people to become empowered. As with other key thinkers, Freire understood that for true participation and empowerment to take place, you have to engage directly with the people being oppressed. As he stated:

> Who are better prepared than the oppressed to understand the terrible significance of an oppressed society? Who suffer the effects of oppression more than the oppressed? Who can better understand the necessity of liberation? (Freire, 1996, p. 27)

Liberation underpinned all of Freire's work and for him this was the most important element of teaching. He believed that 'conscious, creative action and reflection' (Gerhardt, 1994, p. 447) would then help support the social liberation of marginalised and socially excluded people within society. But for this to truly happen professionals have to live alongside and accurately understand the world from the 'oppressed people's point of view which then leads professionals to be able to engage in meaningful dialogue' (Eichteller et al., 2014, p. 46). As Freire (1996, p. 71) wrote:

> How can I dialogue if I regard myself as a case apart from others … ? How can I dialogue if I consider myself to be a member of the in-group of 'pure' men, owners of the truth and knowledge, for whom all non-members are 'these people' or 'the great unwashed'?

By challenging the social position and seeing yourself as equal to the people you are working with, you then build up a dialogical relationship that can be used to bring about *conscientization* (Smith, 2002). Freire (1996) explained this to be when people really understand and become aware of the social structures and power dynamics that keep them oppressed but that they also become conscious of the abilities they have within themselves to change these structures to end this oppression. Critical reflection and social action that came about because of the relationship between people was the most powerful force in changing society in a positive way. Education systems therefore played a key part in *conscientization* and should challenge the *banking* educational system being used around the world whereby the teachers were seen to fill students full of knowledge (Freire, 1996). He highlighted that when this approach is used in education or social work/care practice, people become *objects* that are then educated or helped by *subjects* that always hold the more powerful positions and have control in defining knowledge (Freire, 1996). Learning and development, therefore, must be rooted in the world of the people you are working with and relate to their lives for them to gain full meaning and understanding.

Freire is an important figure in relation to social pedagogy, as he explains that the starting point for liberation has to be a profound love for all human beings and the ability to see and believe in the potential of human beings. As he wrote:

> If I do not love the world – if I do not love life – if I do not love people – I cannot enter into dialogue. (Freire, 1996, p. 71)

This links to the guiding principles and the humanistic value base of social pedagogy, demonstrated in the Diamond Model developed by Eichsteller and Holthoff (2011a). It also requires us to recognise the positions of power and the part we play in oppressive social structures. For Freire our actions are as important as our values and critical reflections. Our words are without meaning if they are not followed up with actions, as he suggests, 'Right thinking is right doing' (Freire, 2001, p. 39).

In order to bring this timeline up to date, the contribution of a number of individuals are important to include. The first is Professor of Social Pedagogy, Claire Cameron, who is a founding member of the Centre for Understanding Social Pedagogy, the Social Pedagogy Professional Association (SPPA) and Deputy Director of the Thomas Coram Research Unit at the University College London Institute of Education. Professor Cameron has been involved in several studies looking at how to develop social pedagogical practice here in the UK, the most well-known being the pilot project aimed at using social pedagogy in the care of *looked after* children living in residential units (the outcome of which is discussed in Chapter 4). She also co-edited one of the first books written in English discussing social pedagogy, entitled *Social Pedagogy and Working with Children and Young People: Where Care and Education Meet* (2011a). As part of the SPPA, Professor Claire Cameron's focus is to help scale up social pedagogy within social work/care in the UK.

Professor Pat Petrie works alongside Professor Claire Cameron and is the Head of the Centre for Understanding Social Pedagogy and a founding member of the SPPA. She has worked on many cross-national projects and during her research into the childcare of school age children across Europe, she became interested in social pedagogy. Due to this she was also involved with the pilot project using social pedagogy in children's residential units. One of the focuses of Professor Petrie's work has been around creativity and the arts and the importance this plays in social pedagogical practice. Along with Helen Chambers she developed the *Learning Framework for Artist Pedagogues* (2009) and has also written a core textbook looking at communication titled *Communication Skills for Working with Children and Young People: Introducing Social Pedagogy* (2011). Both Professor Claire Cameron and Professor Pat Petrie have been instrumental in the development of social pedagogy being used in social work practice and continue to support these developments.

The final two individuals, neither of whom would identify themselves with social pedagogy, but whose core concepts, themes and ideas undoubtedly link, are Ken Robinson and Hilary Cottam. Ken Robinson is an educational advisor and public speaker. Having previously been a teacher he has first-hand experience of our education system and some of the issues within it. His 2006 TED Talk, *Do Schools Kill Creativity?*, is the most watched of all time and has been viewed over 40 million times by people around the world. He has also published a number of books, one of which, titled *Out of Our Minds: Learning to be Creative* (2011), links well to social pedagogy and the work of Professor Pat Petrie around creativity. Ken Robinson discusses the importance of using creativity to unlock potential within people and to challenge and change social structure for the benefit of us all. Like Paulo Freire's key ideas and practice, he offers us three important concepts to work by. The first of these is that we should foster diversity and all learning should be tailored to an individual's needs (in social work/ care this is what we would call person-centred support). Second, in order for people to grow and develop we need to cultivate their curiosity – if we are curious then our learning happens at a deeper level. Finally, to support people in becoming curious, we should use a didactic approach where we are seen as the guide and resource for learning (Robinson, 2011). Again this fits with the key idea of working alongside people and not doing social work *to* people (Petrie, 2011).

The work of social entrepreneur Hilary Cottam has led her to look at creative solutions to social problems across the globe. She has just published her latest book entitled *Radical Help: How Can We Remake the Relationship Between Us and Revolutionise the Welfare State* (2018). In her book and during her TED Talk, she encourages us to think about alternative, creative ways of working within social work/care settings but that this must start with the power of relationships. With a real link to social pedagogy, she writes about how relationships are key for supporting people to unlock their own potential in being able to find long-lasting solutions to problems they are experiencing within their lives. As Beveridge acknowledged in his final report about the design of the welfare state, he had made a grave error in ignoring the part individuals and communities play in providing welfare services and assisting one another (Cottam, 2008).

Conclusion

Even though this has been a brief historical journey, hopefully this chapter has presented the development of social pedagogy ideas, philosophy and practice over the last 300 years. One of the key themes of the chapter has been the important role individuals and the collective play in pushing forward positive social change.

Further Reading

A brief history of social pedagogy:

www.thempra.org.uk/social-pedagogy/historic-developments-in-social-pedagogy/

Social pedagogy: the development of theory and practice:

http://infed.org/mobi/social-pedagogy-the-development-of-theory-and-practice/

SOCIAL PEDAGOGY CONCEPTS

ALI GARDNER

Social Pedagogy

Social pedagogy is essentially concerned with well-being, learning and growth. At the core is a belief that equality should exist between professionals and individuals accessing support and services. Social pedagogy is concerned with both the individual and society and seeks to understand the space between the two in order to connect them in a meaningful manner. By placing relationships at the heart of all engagements, social pedagogues seek to facilitate individuals being included and contributing to the wider society.

The word pedagogy is not a word commonly used in this country but it means education or formal learning. The insertion of the word *social* emphasises the wider process of learning and development across the whole lifespan.

For many people working in social work or social care, these definitions may reflect our own understanding or motivation of working in this sector. Social pedagogy however draws on many strands, including psychology, philosophy, sociology, politics and anthropology, offering a rich theoretical framework that can inform our practice. It avoids promoting or privileging any one method or theory but instead requires a critical engagement with wide-ranging disciplines and theories. As practitioners, this knowledge can be used to support our understanding of each individual and the unique circumstances they bring to each situation. At this point it might be helpful to reflect on Hämäläinen's assertion that,

> … an action is not social pedagogical because certain methods are used but as a consequence of social pedagogical thought. (Hämäläinen, 2003, p. 77)

In order to examine what we mean by social pedagogical thought, we will begin with our first social pedagogical concept.

Haltung is a German word, which roughly translates as mindset or ethos. Social pedagogy relies heavily on authentic engagements with the individuals we work alongside. It firmly asserts that both the professional and personal elements of the practitioner play key roles in the social pedagogical relationship. They are intrinsically interwoven as the 'whole' person is brought to work every day and in every situation. *Haltung*, therefore, becomes a key consideration in our work.

One way of thinking about *Haltung* may be to imagine a compass that guides our actions in life. It is our ethical orientation in practice. The degree of movement of the needle of the compass will vary depending on the beliefs and values shaping us as individuals. It would however be expected, in social pedagogy, that the arrow, at the top of the compass, always points in the same direction, towards profound respect for human dignity. As the map-reader, our magnetic needle remains steady, highlighting our starting position and journey as we approach each situation. In this sense we remain committed to our values and morals in our work, no matter how challenging the terrain or journey may be. We may use the compass at home when deciding whether to walk or take the car on a short journey or whether to buy a more expensive brand of cleaning materials due to our ecological concerns. Likewise, the same compass can be used when working alongside individuals and when we are making considerations relevant to practice. Essentially we are recognising that *Haltung* is not something we adopt for a situation, nor is it something we think about during only our working hours. In order for us to use it effectively we must continually reflect on the use of our compass and check that we are using it with empathy, sensitivity and integrity.

In social work, the inescapable use of self in practice has been well documented (Jones, 2009). Cooper (2012) suggests that the definition of social work must have 'use of self' at its core as social workers use themselves as the instruments of their practice. Similarly, Kaushick (2017) suggests that knowing self is a precondition to knowing others. In social work practice, therefore, it is the conscious use of self that makes this a professional skill rather than a natural or common sense one. The fundamental focus on human interaction in social work means that at every juncture or intervention in our practice, the use of self will be called upon to understand, interpret, analyse, consolidate, reflect and review information.

 **ACTIVITY 3.1**

Use of self in practice

In pairs, think about a personal experience that has influenced your decision to become a social worker. This could have been a positive or negative experience. It could have been something you experienced or observed in someone close to you or in your community or society. This could be a very emotive exercise for some people, so take a moment to check that you feel able and willing to discuss it with your partner.

Describe the experience briefly to your partner. Your partner should then use questions to try to draw out how you have understood the experience, how and why you have interpreted it and analysed it in the way that you have. Your partner should also encourage you to reflect on this experience, checking whether interpretations or analysis have changed over time; and finally, your partner should ask you to identify both the positive and potential negative impact this experience may have on you in supporting another individual in the future.

Hopefully this exercise will have provided you with some reflective space to review an experience and focus on the uniqueness of 'self' when interpreting and analysing a situation. This conscious use of self can support you in the professional task of recognising when, how and why you connect with information and experiences presented by the individuals you work alongside. As we navigate our way through the professional role, balancing issues of choice, capacity and risk, for example, attention to the conscious and positive use of self becomes central to our practice.

Haltung is therefore very much connected with use of self. It represents the authentic relationship that the professional brings to their work. It is reflective of Carl Rogers' core conditions of counselling: congruence, empathetic understanding and unconditional positive regard (Rogers, 1951). It is the insistence upon an emotional connectedness to the work that makes it more than a method or a theory but also about a way of 'being'. Philosopher Eric Mührel (2008) suggests there are two pillars for a social pedagogical *Haltung*: comprehending and regarding.

The notion of *comprehending* highlights the importance of understanding an individual, their way of life and their perspective through dialogue and relationship-based communication. By *regarding*, Mührel refers to accepting the otherness in people who are different from ourselves. It is only by looking beyond our own understanding of the world and stepping into the shoes of others that we can truly respect and accept that which might be strange or different to ourselves. In social work the ability and willingness to take time to comprehend and regard is key to our practice. We must seek to find the uniqueness in individuals in order to avoid reducing them to what we are familiar with. In organisations where assessments and services are increasingly process driven and resources squeezed, it is essential that we are able to remain open and outward looking, in order to understand the specific strengths and needs of individuals, particularly when they do not quite match the specific eligibility wording provided.

Haltung not only refers to our day-to-day interactions with individuals but also connects us with another key aspect of social pedagogy which relates to the wider aim of social justice. Eichsteller and Holthoff (2011a) argue that social pedagogical *Haltung* provides the context for social pedagogy's aims and purpose at the level of community and society (p. 38). It is important, therefore, that we recognise the values shaping legislation, policies, services and practice. This is centrally important as social pedagogy emerges in the UK and provides the basis for our intervention (Coussée et al., 2010). We will return to this point in Chapter 4 as we explore how a social pedagogical narrative is emerging in recent legislation and policy. For the moment, it is important to recognise that the explicit and implicit principles and ethos (*Haltung*) of legislation can play a powerful role in shaping our practice and the relationship between the state and people who access services and support.

Head, Heart and Hands

Central to social pedagogy is the concept of Head, Heart and Hands, a term coined by Swiss social reformer and educator, Pestalozzi (1746–1827). He believed that every individual had the ability to learn and should have the right to education and that this could be achieved through employing the head, heart and hands. He asserted the inseparable nature of all three. The head is related to the intellectual side or the knowledge that we use to understand a situation. As a practitioner the use of the head refers to the knowledge we have and our ability to connect this to information we are given. In social work practice this might relate to knowledge of legislation, policy, theories, processes or available resources. As social workers there is an expectation that we have an appropriate knowledge base in order to support individuals effectively. Pestalozzi suggested that alongside our knowledge or the *head*, one must have a deep respect for humanity. This requires an ability to accept individuals unconditionally and engage at an emotional level with others. Pestalozzi referred to this as the *heart*. In social work it might translate as caring about the work that we undertake and remaining person-centred at all times. Within a social pedagogical approach, this emotional connectedness to one's work is central to every engagement. Practice is essentially driven by passion, compassion and genuine belief in the potential and growth of all individuals.

Social work, whilst recognising the use of self as central to practice, has marginalised language such as heart or love in preference for a discourse surrounding professional expertise (Godden, 2017). Practitioners are expected to employ managed emotions with clear procedurally led boundaries to their relationships to service users. Social pedagogy, on the other hand, welcomes the inclusion of heart and even the notion of *love* as a means of conveying the passion for incorporating human rights and social justice and the emancipatory nature of the work.

Finally, the *hands* symbolise the importance of the practical application of our engagements with individuals. The hands work in two ways within a social pedagogical approach. Firstly, they represent us acting as a consequence of processes, knowledge and information. In working alongside adults, this is likely to involve enabling adults to undertake the practical tasks which 'promote their inclusion, participation, social identity and social competence as a member of society' (Hämäläinen, 2003, p. 76). Secondly, the hands may be viewed as a means of understanding. Brühlmeier (2010) suggests that the practical work with our hands may guide us in understanding what works and what does not. In this sense our direct work with individuals may generate feelings that offer subtler but important connections that inform our practice.

The application of hands within a social pedagogical approach opens up opportunities to apply a range of creative approaches to working alongside individuals, including the arts, physical activities, use and exploration of different environments, advocacy and participation and political engagements. We will return to the notion of creativity and its relevance to social pedagogical practice in the next section.

Smith and Whyte (2008) suggests that Pestalozzi's key concern with social justice led him to asserting the use of Head, Heart and Hands in everyday experiences. In order to educate the whole person, Pestalozzi insisted on the need for equilibrium in all strands. From a social work perspective which also concerns itself centrally with social justice, the Head, Heart and Hands model has great potential, particularly as many of the recent political efforts have been focused on reorganising structures and systems rather than relationships as a means to improve service delivery (Brühlmeier, 2010). Similarly, Ferguson (2008) calls for us to resist pressures of managerialism emanating from neoliberal ideas and to reclaim the profession, based on its formative commitment to values including democracy, participation, justice and equality. Whilst the employment of Head, Heart and Hands is unlikely to offer a panacea to social injustice, it provides practitioners and social work leaders an opportunity to reframe their efforts to reflect values aligned to a more liberal and humane profession that attracted many of them to the work in the first place. As financial and workload pressures intensify and underpinning values of social justice become more fragile, it becomes increasingly important that the fundamental aims of social work are protected and promoted.

Creativity

You may have started to notice the frequent use of the following quote from Hämäläinen (2003, p. 77) in this book, 'an action is not social pedagogical because certain methods are used but as a consequence of social pedagogical thought'. There are no apologies for the overuse of this quote that fundamentally guides our understanding of social pedagogical practice. Whilst it may appear somewhat circular, it invites a more analytical, critical, curious and creative engagement with one's practice. As a consequence of employing Head, Heart and Hands and resisting the one-dimensional instrumental or procedural approach, the practitioner is encouraged to think more laterally and speculatively as a way of moving beyond the obvious. Clearly, competency to apply legislation, systems, policies, theories and methods is central to the social work role but the ability to interpret 'rules' and select one particular method instead of another requires creativity.

From a social pedagogical perspective, creativity can mean many things and be applied in different ways. The notion of creativity is often associated with a specific talent, skill or personality trait and it is probably fair to suggest that social pedagogy has attracted and ben-efited from individuals who identify with this notion of creativity. Hatton (2013) highlights a number of creative arts-based projects with a social pedagogical influence leading to the pro-motion of health and well-being and increased self-esteem, confidence and empowerment. However, the notion of creativity in the context of social pedagogy and social work can extend beyond arts-based activity. Fundamentally, creativity starts with a deep respect for and emo-tional connectedness to the individuals we work alongside. Jackson and Burgess (2005) suggest that creativity comes through the use of self, genuine warmth and empathy. A report from the National Foundation for Educational Research (NFER, 2006) identified creativity as encompass-ing four key characteristics: using imagination, pursuing purpose, originality and judging value. In this model, the goal is ultimately to find imaginative solutions to solve human problems or challenges. Importantly, however, it is a co-produced process with a very nuanced application of creativity. In the first instance, the practitioner needs to understand the situation. They need to be able to see the world in the way the individual sees it. The first role therefore is to cre-ate the best conditions for the individual to reveal their stories. Moving through this process together enables the practitioner to draw on relevant knowledge, legislation, policies, theories and resource/support options. The co-productive nature of this process lays the foundations for a creative rather than linear or formulaic approach to problem solving. The practitioner is able to use their knowledge, understanding and imagination to consider a wide range of options. The application of imagination is clearly linked to tangible outcomes for the individual or situation. Essentially, it is the knowing of the individual and the given situation that enables practitioners to move beyond a technical or procedural approach to problem solving.

It is not uncommon for practitioners to feel that their creativity is being stifled by procedures, lack of time and resources (Jackson and Burgess, 2005). Vygotsky (2004, in Hatton, 2013, p. 31) captures a common experience for many practitioners in stating 'creation is difficult, the drive to create does not always coincide with the capacity to create'. There will also be times in practice when the decision-making process needs to be more instrumental, for example in car-rying out legal duties which may not be welcomed by the individuals they are imposed upon. Similarly, current organisational cultures have been found to lead social workers to adopt a defensive approach to their practice (Whittaker and Havard, 2016). Whilst none of the above factors justifies the absence of creativity, it is clear that creativity is more than a technique or approach but is linked to wider aims of co-production, inclusion and social justice.

The Three Ps

Social pedagogy places key emphasis on relationships as a critical resource in our work with individuals, groups and communities. Recognising the potential of using this inner resource is very much at the forefront of good social pedagogical practice. At the same time, social pedagogy acknowledges the complex nature of relationships and using them effectively in practice. The Three Ps – Professional, Personal and Private – (Jappe, 2010) offer a reflexive framework which allows practitioners to understand and manage these three aspects of the self when working alongside individuals. The *professional* strand of the relationship is fundamentally based on the purpose of our engagement with an individual. This may be as a consequence of the law, policy or procedures within the agency. In order to manage the relationship effectively, we will draw upon knowledge, research, practice evidence and theory in the connected field. The theory may include for example our understanding of communication or theory related to emotion or attachment for example. This knowledge is key to informing how we approach and engage with individuals. It is person-centred and requires a commitment to understanding the individual and calls upon our *Haltung*, as discussed earlier in the chapter. Importantly, the *professional* strand recognises the value of inserting the *personal* strand in our practice but seeks to manage this application in a professional manner. As social pedagogy purposefully focuses on building relationships, it recognises the value of sharing a sense of who we are as individuals in working alongside others. A willingness to use our personality and engage in relationships which acknowledge the importance of recognising both strengths and flaws and seeking to reduce hierarchies is key to good social pedagogical practice. If we are committed to a relationship-based approach to our professional work, then we must also attend to the complex nature of relationships and how they operate. One key ingredient to a relationship is the notion of reciprocity, a need to give as well as receive. Thompson (2016), in her research with older people, found that participants yearned for opportunities to reciprocate and that the ability to do so impacted positively on their spiritual well-being. Relationships, by nature, are two-way processes, in which both parties give and receive in order for the relationship to develop. In social work, Thompson (2016) noted the absence of attention to reciprocity in the assessment process for older people. Furthermore, Saleeby (2006) suggests that reciprocity is consistent with a strength-based approach and in turn, promotes resilience. The bureaucratic and sometimes, risk averse nature of social work practice often leaves little room for a relationship-based approach to the work. If, however, we recognise that relationships are one of our most critical resources (Cottam, 2018) then surely promoting reciprocity is, as Thompson (2016) suggests, 'entirely compatible with the social work endeavour' (p. 346).

It could be argued therefore that the insertion of self in working positively alongside others is inescapable and furthermore, the absence of the *personal* prevents us from practising in a professional manner. The *personal*, however, can only ever be used effectively if we can set the boundary with our *private* self. The *private* strand refers to those aspects of the self that we do not share with individuals. They remain outside of our work with individuals. Managing this boundary between the personal and private requires good self-awareness and reflective skills. We may choose to keep aspects of our lives in the private domain if we have not processed them fully. For example, one practitioner may refer to having a partner or a child with ease whereas another may feel this information needs to remain in their private domain. The reasons for this choice may also be highly complex and multilayered. Likewise, a practitioner may decide to share an experience of change, transition or loss, for example, with one individual but not another. In this scenario the practitioner is focusing on the motivation, purpose and benefit of sharing the information and using professional judgement and integrity to arrive at this decision. Importantly, the decision is specific to *this* interaction, with *this* individual, in *these* circumstances and would need to be reviewed and revised again in the next situation. Again there is no formula or set approach instructing what can and cannot be shared, but our *moral compass*, discussed earlier in this chapter, governed by our *Haltung* is navigating us through the Three Ps. The important point is that aspects of the personal must only be shared where there is a clear purpose and benefit to the individual and where the practitioner feels comfortable in doing so. Social pedagogy is about being with others, forming relationships and being present and authentic. This is brought to life by our *Haltung* rather than any process or assessment form. Relationship-based approaches and the use of self in practice support our engagements and assessments when working alongside individuals as well as supporting them to create and facilitate opportunities to feel valued and valuable.

Common Third

Social pedagogues are continually searching for ways to enhance relationships and communication. The Common Third, a Danish concept (Lihme, 1988), is central to social pedagogy practice and focuses on activities to strengthen relationships between the individual and the practitioner. In connecting with another person through the shared activity, the focus becomes the experience of togetherness and distracts from any power or hierarchies that may exist. Importantly, there is no expert in the activity and the focus on learning something together facilitates a more equal relationship. The choice of activity has to be shared by both the individual and the practitioner and the notion of choosing, therefore, paves the way for a more co-productive experience. The exact nature of the activity is not important. It could be cooking a pancake, learning how to do a hand massage or fixing a bike. One of the students developing social pedagogy as part of her practice at our university agreed to learn how to speak in different accents with a young person she was working with. The social work student had suggested the use of the Common Third and asked the young person for some ideas. The young person had always wanted to learn different accents, so the student agreed and together they started to practise. This allowed them to talk about many important issues whilst talking in different accents. The experience was equally challenging for both parties and provided a genuine connectedness in their relationship. On reflection, the student identified how the activity had allowed a more equal relationship as neither were the expert and both could teach and learn from the other at different points. She also reported having fun with the young person and that it enabled them to connect in a much more meaningful manner than would have been possible using traditional approaches.

The activity becomes the symbol of the relationship. It allows both parties to focus on the shared activity rather than concentrating so intently on the other person. This allows the relationship to strengthen more naturally and can be a less threatening experience for individuals who are repeatedly required to share information or aspects of themselves with several professionals. This will not be a new concept to many practitioners in social work and social care. As a social worker, I remember using similar approaches such as taking a ball in the back of the car to kick around in the park whilst talking to a young person or meeting at a local animal sanctuary to look around and learn about the animals. In each situation I was aiming to reduce the power or intensity of the experience and to use the activity as a focus or distraction as required. Although I had not framed this as the Common Third, I was aware that the experience supported and strengthened the relationship. Foster parents will commonly speak of naturally using this approach to support the development of relationships when children experience the daunting move into a new house with strangers and little if any choice about the whole process. As with any model, framework or approach, it is beneficial to engage both naturally and analytically when applying it to practice. The Common Third encourages the practitioner, through reflection, to focus on clarifying the purpose and inclusion of the individual along with evaluating the impact it has on the aim of strengthening the relationship.

CASE EXAMPLE 3.1

Safe Zone is a project set up by the International Rescue Committee (IRC) in Greece supporting unaccompanied minors. During a field visit to the project, Hadi (2018) spent time with staff and 30 boys originating from Iraq, Libya, Syria, Pakistan, Bangladesh and Afghanistan living at the project. The role of the staff is to support the boys' upbringing and to involve them in the drafting of a *best interests assessment* (Article 3, UNCRC). Importantly, Hadi found, the assessment did not focus on data collation of histories and legal issues of status or residence but was directed by the boys and the information they chose to share, the emphasis being on the present and its relation to their future. Hadi found that Common Third activities were used to connect the boys to the staff team, each other and the wider community. He noted that the sharing of everyday activities led to more equal relationships between the worker and the boys, who were viewed as being resourceful and played a significant part in shaping the environment and activities. The boys were involved in planning activities, purchasing or making equipment enabling them to build the relationships, self-confidence and new skills. He found that the preparation and sharing of food helped to connect the boys to their identity and culture and built an ethos of care and respect throughout the

(Continued)

(Continued)

project. Hadi concluded that the activities became something more than an end in themselves but instead a mechanism for the boys to strengthen relationships, develop new capabilities and identity, direct their own best interests assessments and experience a sense of connection with the group and the community.

Reflection

The power of the Common Third is illustrated beautifully here. Supporting the boys to be a part of something that is shared yet separate from themselves enables them to build relationships naturally. The activities connect the individuals without intruding on the personal aspects of their lives. The choice and control of what and when to share information remains with the boys. As discussed earlier in the chapter, the activity becomes the symbol of the relationship which can develop more naturally. Furthermore, the purposeful nature of the activities such as sport, cooking, creating and learning positively contribute to the boys' well-being in both the present and their futures.

Reflection

The ability to continually reflect is essential for all social pedagogues. As I am sure you are starting to see, there is no manual or process to guide social pedagogy practice. As Hämäläinen (2003, p. 77) suggests our actions are as a 'consequence of our social pedagogical thought'. It is important therefore that practitioners attend to their social pedagogical thought in order to review, evaluate and revise actions. Due to the nature of social care/work practice, it is not always possible to carefully plan interactions and there is an expectation that practitioners can respond to unpredictable situations with professionalism and integrity. This requires the ability to reflect as situations emerge, whilst we are *in the thick of it* and again after the event when emotion and urgency may have lowered. Schon (2016) referred to this as reflecting *in-action* (during the event) and *on-action* (after the event). Similarly, Greenaway (1992) offers the four state reviewing model incorporating facts, feelings, findings and futures. In both models there is an acknowledgement that feelings and emotions feature in our work both as practitioners and in the individuals we work alongside and at times can distract us from our focus. Ingram (2013) notes the uneasy relationship professional social work has traditionally had with emotion, arguing, however, that emotions and rational decision-making are compatible and necessary. Similarly, Munro (2011) highlighted the centrality of social work relationships, acknowledging the importance of practitioners being able to identify their own emotional responses and those of the individuals they are working alongside.

Both models address how we respond to situations at the time but importantly how we rewind, process and learn from the experiences after the event. Key educational philosopher John Dewey (1859–1952) first introduced the notion of reflection within experiential learning as part of his work around social change and educational reform. Although the exact location of this quote is unclear, he is believed to have commonly used the phrase, 'we do not learn from experience but from reflecting on that experience'. Using reflective tools in practice such as the two described by Schon and Greenaway above allows the practitioner to consciously review their *Haltung*, use of the Three Ps and the value of adopting Common Third activities. In a sense, it promotes both the natural and analytical application of theory which is central to social pedagogical practice.

Learning Zone

The Learning Zone model suggested by Senninger (2000, in Eichsteller and Holthoff, 2017) provides a useful framework not only to understand the starting point for an individual but also as a tool to support the learning process and development of individuals. The model is made up of three domains as indicated in Figure 3.1 (see next page). Underpinning the model is the assumption that growth and development can only take place in the learning zone and that it is here where an individual is required to reach in order to learn and slowly expand abilities. It is the place where individuals live out curiosity and make new discoveries (Eichsteller and Holthoff, 2017). Before reaching the learning zone, however, we need to explore, with individuals, their comfort zone. This is the place where everything feels safe and familiar for the individual. The comfort zone should present no risks to the individual. It is a safe haven to which individuals can return and process information and reflect on experiences. As with every zone, they are unique to the individual and therefore must be understood through the lens of the individual. For example, sitting down with the family and enjoying a home-cooked meal may be at the heart of some people's comfort zone. This however could be very different for a child entering a foster home who has never sat at a table and shared a meal. This could present real panic for the child. Imagine a foster carer, referring to their own comfort zone and planning a welcome dinner for the young person with the extended family as an attempt to provide comfort and security at the start of his/her move. Meanwhile the child has quickly found him/herself in the panic zone, where any learning or sense of comfort is blocked by a sense of fear. All the child's energy is used in managing and controlling their anxiety. Without first understanding what it is that presents comfort to the young person, it is impossible to move to the learning zone where growth and development can start to happen. Senninger (2000, in Eichsteller and Holthoff, 2017) states the importance of the model as a means of supporting the individual to move towards the edges of the learning zone. This is the place where managed risks can be taken which creates the belief and confidence in the individual that further steps can be taken. Viscott (2003) suggests that this requires a temporary loss of security to enable the process of growth. The learning zone therefore is inextricably linked with risk and therefore reinforces the need for children to experience situations which require a certain amount of trust in the unknown, in order for personal development to happen.

Figure 3.1
Learning Zone Model

(Thempra 2017a, reproduced
with kind permission of
ThemPra)

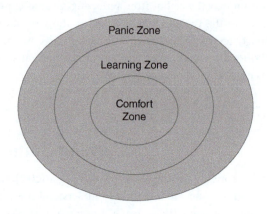

 **ACTIVITY 3.2**

Reflecting on your learning zone

On a piece of paper, draw the figure above giving yourself enough space to write inside each zone. First start with the comfort zone. Write down anything that you would include in this zone. For example, you might find comfort in being curled up on the sofa watching TV or walking in the park. Maybe you find comfort in a chocolate bar or spending time with your pet. As discussed above, it will be different for us all. Once you have completed the general comforts, you should now think of a situation where you have experienced a level of panic when taking on a new challenge. This could be something in your professional life such as your first week on a social work placement or it could be learning a new skill such as driving a car. Try to focus on a situation which evoked a high level of emotion for you and describe some of the feelings in the panic zone.

Next you should focus on returning to the comfort zone. Is there anything else you would like to add in relation to the example you have picked. For example, if you used your social work placement, the comfort zone might have included being back at the office with your colleagues, a walk to the shop at lunchtime or driving home at the end of the day. Try to focus on what represented comfort to you in the situation.

Once you have focused on these comforts, think about how you could change the situation to take you to the learning zone, without falling into the panic zone. Using the reflective models discussed above, can you identify changes to the experience that would allow growth and development as opposed to fear and feelings of being immobilised. Remember that this may include taking some risks and a level of trust in the unknown, but how can you prepare yourself for these steps?

In summary, this exercise helps demonstrate the uniqueness of learning zones. If you share your model with a colleague, I am sure you will quickly recognise this. Reminding yourself of your own comfort zones and giving yourself permission to return to them is a central part of the learning process. This is the place where real reflection can happen and provide the confidence and energy to step into the learning zone. It is also useful to think about your own models in relation to the individuals we work alongside. Firstly, so that we take time to understand their perspective and experience rather than only deferring to our own interpretations. Secondly, identifying with the intensity of the emotion that others may experience. This is where empathy can take place. You may not fully understand how and why others feel a certain way in some situations but you can identify with the emotion that is evoked as a consequence. This in turn will enable you to support the individual in returning to their comfort zone and building again to move towards the edge of their learning zone.

Zone of Proximal Development

Russian psychologist Vygotsky (1978), in his work with children, coined the term Zone of Proximal Development. He argued that learning was most successful in a social context, whereby individuals were supported by someone who is more advanced such as a teacher, mentor or social pedagogue. Vygotsky defined the Zone of Proximal Development as:

> ... the distance between the actual developmental level as determined by independent problem solving and the level of potential development as determined through problem solving under adult guidance or in collaboration with more capable peers. (1978, p. 86)

Vygotsky believed there were things a child could do alone and some they were unable to do. He was however interested in the space between in which there was potential for the child to learn but with the assistance of a mentor. This space sits firmly in the learning zone as discussed above, and the role of the mentor or social pedagogue is to guide the learning. Schwartz (2001) stressed the importance on this learning being a mutual process, where possible, rather than a teacher instructing the child on how to act or behave. Using the Common Third for example could support the learning process. Unlocking and realising the potential of the child is very much at the heart of the Zone of Proximal Development and as such relies heavily on profound respect and belief in the individuals we work alongside. Although Vygotsky did not refer specifically to scaffolding, a concept introduced by Wood et al. (1976), it is closely related to the Zone of Proximal Development. Wood et al. (1976) refer to scaffolding being the support offered by the mentor during the learning process, just as scaffolding is erected around a building during construction, and then removed as the child develops independence in that aspect and the building can stand alone. There are many ways this approach can be used in practice and it draws upon many of the concepts that have already been discussed in this chapter. From a UK perspective, the social work role can be viewed as focusing primarily on care rather than education. Whilst the structural and operational configuration of care and education varies considerably throughout the world, it is important to recognise that the notion of learning rather than educating is central to social pedagogical practice and is compatible and necessary within the UK social care context as it is in other countries.

Relational Universe

The Relational Universe is a useful concept in understanding and supporting relationship-based practice. Fundamentally, it acknowledges that as human beings, from the moment we are born, we are connected to various individuals. For many of us these connections and relationships will deepen and extend to include others as we proceed through life. For all of us, there is no choice in our immediate experience of our universe and this may be experienced as entirely positive and unproblematic. For others this may not be the case and could ultimately lead to professionals intervening to disrupt natural connections and reconfiguring the child's universe. Understandably, this is a traumatic experience for children as the connection has been established and the estranged parent remains part of the child's universe. Removing a child from a parent will not necessarily break the gravitational pull towards that parent but instead can lead to anger and confusion as decisions are made without the child's permission. Clearly, there may be good reason and legal requirements for this removal but the parent remains part of the child's universe and in many cases a central point of reference in their lives. As professionals, it is therefore important to recognise that the physical removal of a parent from day-to-day life does not automatically lead to an emotional removal from the child's universe. Ignoring or dismissing the connection of this parent on the basis of the relationship being problematic, destructive or even dangerous is not necessarily helpful for the child in developing new relationships and ultimately their future interdependence (Carter and Eichsteller, 2017). In social care, there is great emphasis placed on the notion of independence, whether that be supporting a young person leaving care or an older person leaving hospital to live at home. As human beings, we largely strive to be *interdependent*, engaging in reciprocal relationships that offer a sense of belonging as well as contributing (Rothuizen and Harbo, 2017). The Relational Universe reminds us of the importance of all relationships whether they are positive, problematic, distant or even toxic. Returning to the example of a child being removed from a parent, Carter and Eichsteller (2017) stress the importance of focusing on the assets rather than the deficits of all individuals in the child's relational universe. Furthermore, one must avoid the exclusion of other individuals such as a grandparent or relatives on the basis that they may not be ideal. Clearly this will not be possible in some cases, but excluding a person from caring for or physically being with the child must not lead to erasing them from the child's universe. It is the role of the professional to pursue the connections in whatever way possible even if that can only mean acknowledging their presence and connection to the child. Finally, there could be a perceived tension with legislative requirements whereby social workers believe they are acting in the child's best interest vis-a-vis Section 1 of the Children Act (1989). Conversely, Article 8 of the Human Rights Act (1998) clearly states the right of every individual to respect for private and family life. This is a good example of how we employ the Head, Heart and Hands in navigating our way through such issues in a social pedagogical manner. Article 8 of the Human Rights Act (1998) clearly requires professionals to respect individuals' privacy and family life but as this is a *qualified* rather than *absolute* right, there may be a legitimate reason (legally and/or morally) to interfere with this right. However, the spirit and principles underpinning human rights and the Act itself should continue to be observed despite the need to interfere. The skilled practitioner applies knowledge (the head) regarding legal requirements alongside an in-depth under-standing of the child's relational universe. The heart, through an emotional connectedness with her/his work, enables the practitioner to engage with what is important to the child and what is possible in terms of practice. The complexity of such situations more often than not requires a creative rather than procedural approach to balance competing yet equally valid priorities (the hand).

The Diamond Model

The Diamond Model (Figure 3.2, see next page) brings together many of the concepts dis-cussed above and symbolises the key principles underpinning social pedagogy. Eichsteller and Holthoff (2012) developed the metaphor of a diamond, often perceived as being pre-cious and sparkly, to articulate the basis upon which we engage with others at all times, with profound respect and recognition of the rich knowledge, skills and abilities they bring with them. They suggest that diamonds, like humans, are not always shiny and polished but all have the potential to be. Focusing on four key aims of well-being and happiness, holistic learning, relationships and empowerment, social pedagogy can support individuals to recog-nise, identify and direct this potential.

Figure 3.2

The Diamond Model

(Eichstellar and Holthoff, 2012, reproduced with the kind permission of ThemPra)

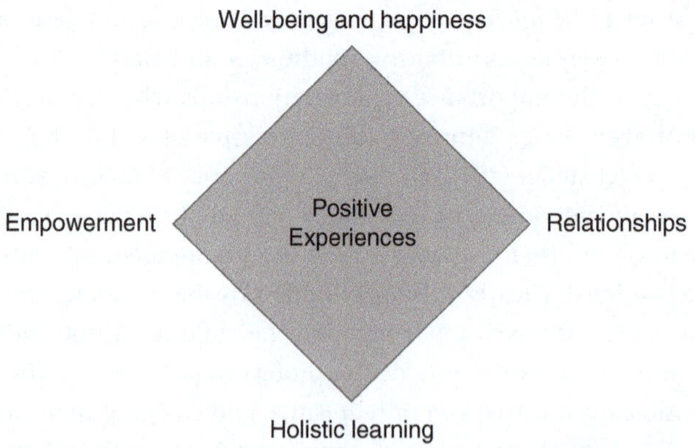

Well-being and happiness

Empowerment

Positive Experiences

Relationships

Holistic learning

Well-being and happiness

The overarching aim of social pedagogical practice is to promote well-being and happiness. The concept of well-being is frequently used in child and adult legislation and policy narrative and is therefore familiar to social work and care. Attending to a more present state of happiness in working alongside individuals may be equally as important. Recognising one's happiness and the cause of it may play a significant part in directing a more sustainable and positive physical, mental, emotional and social well-being. Focusing on happiness and the experiences that lead to this emotional state reminds the practitioner of the highly individualised and context-specific nature of happiness and furthermore can support a more highly responsive approach to achieving more sustainable well-being.

Holistic learning

Social pedagogy firmly asserts the importance of learning at all stages and in all aspects of life. Recognising one's potential supports the first step of development and learning. Social pedagogy is about creating opportunities and spaces for the learning to happen. This is different from a teaching role whereby the expert is providing the answers or solutions. Learning in this sense is unique and self-directed. The role of the social pedagogue is to facilitate individuals in accessing a sense of potential and walking alongside the individual as the learning takes place. Drawing on some of the earlier concepts discussed, including the Common Third, the Learning Zone and the Zone of Proximal Development, helps to clarify the role of the social pedagogue, which is to experience and share and encourage learning wherever possible.

Relationships

The Diamond Model recognises the centrality of the relationship and insists upon the importance of practitioners adopting a relationship-based approach to all of their work.

As discussed earlier in the chapter, the use of self in practice is a critical resource which paves the way for learning and securing future relationships. The practitioner can offer an experience of relating positively to support this development. The Three Ps framework provides a useful way to explore and reflect on the different strands. It requires highly tuned skills of professional judgement and integrity in order for us to manage professional relationships which can benefit from the insertion of the personal in a safe and positive manner.

Empowerment

Experiencing a sense of control in life is fundamental to our well-being, and feeling out of control often immobilises learning and moving forward. As we noted in the Learning Zone model above, the feeling of losing control and panic present major obstacles. Social pedagogy is therefore centrally concerned with individuals making sense of their own universe rather than being instructed as to what changes are required and how they can be made. In many ways, this can be a longer process, as the individual takes ownership for their learning and relationships. Social pedagogy recognises the importance of balancing aims of independence with interdependence and therefore guards against professionalised or procedure-driven responses that tend to focus on *fixing* a problem with little attention to the ownership or sustainability of solutions.

Positive experiences

The Diamond Model positions positive experiences at the centre of the diamond. Eichsteller and Holthoff (2012) suggest that positive experiences become an important vehicle in meeting the four core aims. Trevithick (2003), who writes prolifically on relationship-based practice, strongly supports the notion of energising experiences to develop self-worth, confidence and belief in one's own potential. Clearly, a positive experience that leads to a sense of happiness or satisfaction enhances one's well-being. Similarly, experiencing positive relationships and a sense of care and regard has a significant impact on one's self-worth. It is through these positive experiences that future learning and capacity-building become more likely and take a person nearer to a sense of ownership, pride and empowerment.

ACTIVITY 3.3

Social pedagogy in practice

There are elements of social pedagogy that will be familiar in many aspects of social care and social work but the following example demonstrates how a social pedagogical approach can be adopted and applied in practice. Read the example

(Continued)

(Continued)

and answer the questions at the end to reflect on your understanding of the key concepts discussed above.

Wellbeing Teams

Wellbeing Teams were established in 2015 by Helen Sanderson and are currently operating in a number of areas across the country. Wellbeing Teams work with commissioners and other care providers to deliver support to adults with care and support needs under the Care Act (2014). The model aims to provide person-centred care and support to people and to connect them with their community. Recognising the pressure on home care services in the UK, Sanderson wanted to change the way services were being delivered to people and to those who were delivering the services. The teams are small and neighbourhood-based and provide a flexible and responsive approach to meeting individual needs, focusing on outcomes and building up support networks. The concept of self-management means that planning and decisions are made close to those receiving and delivering the support rather than in a hierarchal structure.

The following extract is from an interview conducted by social care magazine *Care Management Matters* with Helen Sanderson about the development of Wellbeing Teams. A link to the full interview can be found at the end of this chapter.

> The challenge was to create a different way of delivering support for people at home that is truly person-centred, where they have choice and control, and it's delivered by an engaged, happy workforce. Having choice and control matters to our Wellbeing Workers as well as people using services, and having friends at work is critical to productivity and happiness. That is why we build choice, control and relationships into the DNA of Wellbeing Teams.

Wellbeing Teams have six core values: compassion, responsibility, collaboration, curiosity, creativity and flourishing. Helen explained, 'Central to this is the context in which the teams operate and most importantly, the headline purpose of the team is to support and connect people with their community.' `She continued:

> Teams are built on the following: Relationships are everything; Wellbeing; Person-centred support; Bringing our whole selves to work; Appreciation and feedback; Taking risks and learning; Celebrating; Trust; and Openly sharing information.
>
> …
>
> Aligning values and practice is a key step in enabling a coherent and stable team culture to evolve.

Questions

1   Can you identify any of the concepts discussed in this chapter that could be applied to the operation of Wellbeing Teams?
2   How do you think this way of working benefits the individuals who receive support and those who deliver it?
3   Do you think there are any obstacles to working in this way and if so how might they be addressed?

Summary

I am sure you could identify a number, if not all the social pedagogical concepts in the extract. Whilst Sanderson does not use the terminology of social pedagogy, it is clear that her philosophy, values and practices align with this approach. You may have identified a range of benefits to those receiving support but hopefully you could also see the benefits to those delivering the support, who report feeling more connected and valued in their roles as they are included in planning and reviewing care and support as well as delivering it. In terms of the challenges, you might have considered the risks of staff leaving having developed positive personal relationships with individuals and their families. You may also have thought about risks presented to individuals if staff are off sick or on leave and the team is only small. You may have been concerned about the absence of a traditional manager overlooking the work of the team. Whilst it is necessary to acknowledge obstacles and challenges in new ways of working, it is important that we do not allow them to stifle creativity and taking risks to try things differently. The only justification for keeping things the same is if the *same* is working. Unfortunately, a quick glance at government reports and research relating to adult social care would suggest this is not the case. A recent parliamentary briefing report (House of Commons, 2018) highlighted significant funding pressures due to a combination of growing and ageing populations with increasingly complex social and health care needs. The report also noted the increasingly precarious position of care providers.

Conclusion

In this chapter we have explored some of the key social pedagogical concepts. For many practitioners and students, the philosophy and values underpinning the concepts will not necessarily be new or groundbreaking in their content; furthermore they closely reflect the key values and ethical principles upon which the social work profession is based (BASW, 2012). The concepts, however, encourage a more analytical engagement with values and practice. They require a different engagement with individuals that explicitly recognises the educational aspect of the social work/care task with a clear focus on not only helping people to survive in difficult circumstances but also promoting people's individual functioning, inclusion, participation and social identity. Social pedagogical actions are therefore closely linked to emancipatory goals in which individuals are supported to attain and to maintain the experience of meaning and dignity in their lives. Clearly, the political and economic context within which social work takes places is highly relevant and social workers will continue to experience frustration and restriction in their role as they navigate their way through ever increasing bureaucratic landscapes. Challenging and influencing the structural factors impacting on individuals that prevent their inclusion within society is central to social pedagogical practice and reinforces the need for practitioners to continue checking and questioning the ethical themes upon which their work is based.

The concepts can therefore inform, support and explain social pedagogical actions as a consequence of social pedagogical thought.

Further Reading

You can access more information about self-managing teams by following this link:

www.caremanagementmatters.co.uk/feature/self-managing-homecare/

There are a number of useful resources on the following website relating to the core concepts discussed in this chapter:

www.thempra.org.uk

THE DEVELOPMENT OF SOCIAL PEDAGOGY IN CHILDREN, YOUNG PEOPLE AND FAMILIES SOCIAL WORK

LOWIS CHARFE

This chapter will focus on how social pedagogy has been developing within the area of social work practice related to children, young people and their families. It will explore some of the key ideas and values underpinning this area of social work and consider their alignment with social pedagogical theory. In addition, the chapter will provide an overview of developments and practice examples from various organisations throughout the UK.

Theoretical Approaches to Practice

Before exploring the practical implementation of social pedagogy within this field of social work, it is worth discussing the dominant discourses that influence and direct child and families social work and identify the commonalities with social pedagogy where they arise. British social work has a long history and tradition of advocacy, rights, participation and relationship-based practice, all of which have been at the heart of the social work profession. With regard to relational ways of working, there is a wealth of theories and research that underpin and highlight the importance of such an approach within child and families social work practice (Trevithick, 2014a). These range from theories such as Bowlby and Howe's attachment theories, the child development theories of Vygotsky, Piaget and Brunner, to the work of Hughes in relation to the psychological treatment of children who have suffered trauma, through to the work of neuroscientists such as Sigal and Damasio demonstrating the neurological impact of positive relationships on the brain.

The research and theories mentioned above could be identified as one of the factors that have facilitated a growing resurgence around the importance of relationship-based practice. Many social work academics and practitioners have noted the increasing absence of this approach in modern social work practice (Bilson and Martin, 2016; Ruch et al., 2010; Trevithick, 2014a), following a number of high profile cases, attracting media attention which in turn has led to reactive government responses. Consequently, social workers and other professionals working with children, young people and their families have been directed towards adopting a *rational–technical approach* as described by Professor Eileen Munro (2011, cited in Trevithick, 2014a, p. 1), in which notions of accountability, safeguarding and risk management dominate practice (Ruch et al., 2010).

This approach sees current social work practice being directed to concentrate on assessing needs, identifying or investigating problems and developing plans with identified goals. It often ignores relational aspects of social work practice which are seen as a by-product of the work undertaken by a social worker. Due to the amount of policies, procedures, standardised assessment frameworks and forms, Trevithick (2014a) argues that social workers no longer use critical analytical skills but rather focus on the collection of data and information. She argues that this leads to rational thought whereby the complexities of human behaviour, human feelings and the lived experience of the child, young person and the family being assessed are often ignored. Munro (2011, cited in Trevithick, 2014a, p. 1) in her review of the child protection systems in England, stated that the loss of relationship-based work 'seriously hinders the quality and effectiveness of social work'. Arguably, the heart has been lost out of modern social work at the expense of focusing on how to keep children and young people safe by trying to assess and eliminate all risks.

The Brazilian educationalist and key thinker Paulo Freire (1970) argued that marginalised people are disempowered and they are often seen as, and believe themselves to be, the problem that needs fixing. It could be argued that the point Freire is making can be seen in modern child and families social work here in the UK. As Munro (2011, cited in Trevithick, 2014a, p. 1) has stated, and as noted above, this area of social work has taken a rational–technical approach where families are seen as being the problem that the professional social worker needs to fix. A clear example of this can be seen in the Troubled Families Programme launched in 2015, which aimed to identify and support the most disadvantaged families, who were deemed to have multiple and complex problems. The title alones conveys a sense of disempowered families needing the expertise of professional intervention.

Another important area of development over the last 30 years, which links to social pedagogy, has been around children's participation and rights. This is linked directly to the United Nations Convention on the Rights of the Child (UNCRC) (1989), which sets out a duty and focus on children's voices being heard and children participating in decisions about their own lives. At the same time, the UK government brought into force the biggest and most fundamental piece of legislation relating to children and young people, the Children Act (1989).

This laid the foundation for all child welfare, participation and children's rights services with its guiding principles that the welfare of the child must be paramount and the child's voice must be listened to. The articulation of the legal principles embedded within the Children Act (1989), alongside a growing discourse of participation and children's rights linked to relational practices, is clearly aligned to the philosophy underpinning a social pedagogical approach.

Application of Social Pedagogy in Practice

People are often surprised to learn that here in the UK, Scotland has historical links with Northern European welfare policies which are based on social pedagogical ideas from Scandinavian countries. Stephens (2013, p. 27) states that 'social pedagogues apply pedagogical solutions to social problems' and that the upbringing of children and the part communities play in this is important (Smith, 2012). Here the use of social pedagogy to address a social issue can be clearly seen in the Scottish Children's Hearings System. This is an excellent example of the influence of social pedagogical practice in Scotland. In 1961, the Kilbrandon Committee was tasked with reviewing and updating the youth justice system in Scotland and in parts this was to assert its independence from England as it had gained control from the UK parliament and was able to implement its own legal and education systems (Muncie and Goldson, 2006). In developing the new youth justice system, the committee took ideas from Europe and in particular Scandinavian countries (Asquith et al., 2005). The committee wanted to look at alternative ways of providing youth justice that were distinctly different from England, who, at that point, had taken a more punitive approach to dealing with children who broke the law (Muncie and Goldson, 2006).

The Kilbrandon Report made recommendations that can be clearly linked to the key principles of social pedagogy (Asquith et al., 2005; Smith, 2012). These included the notion of the importance of a child's upbringing and the important part a community played in this, rather than this being solely the responsibility of the parent. Social competency was also seen as key, helping children to reach their full potential, and links directly to Karl Mager's definition that the aim of any social pedagogical practice was the 'theory of all personal, social and moral education' (translated by Gabriel Thomas, cited in Cameron and Moss, 2011a, p. 8). The view that education should be seen in the broadest sense and aimed at supporting a child's holistic development was therefore fundamental as well as helping children become an active part of their community. To meet these aims, Kilbrandon made a radical proposal in that he 'proposed a new field organisation, a Department of Social Education staffed by social workers but located within an expanded education department to support these recommendations' (Smith, 2012, p. 49).

The formation of a new government department did not become a reality unfortunately, but many of the Kilbrandon recommendations led to the Social Work (Scotland) Act (1968).

This forced a complete overhaul of the youth justice system and set out the framework for the Children's Hearings System (Smith, 2012). The new system was based on the welfare of children rather than punishment, early intervention, minimal contact with formal welfare agencies, and the importance of decriminalising and destigmatising children by removing them from the criminal justice system was at its heart (Asquith, 2006; McAra, 2012). These key ideas formed the *Haltung* for the Children's Hearings Systems and were clearly linked to social pedagogical philosophy. This new youth justice system also had a wider impact in that social pedagogical principles began to be embedded into other areas of children's services via the Children in Scotland agency. Unfortunately, as with England, Scotland has not been immune to the moral panics around youth crime, as we have seen the erosion of the social pedagogical and welfare principles of the Children's Hearings System as more punitive measures focusing on reducing risk, controlling children and punishing negative behaviour have replaced them (McAra, 2012).

In England things have taken a while longer to develop into practice. Within university settings there has been an academic interest in social pedagogy since the 1990s (Kornbeck, 2009), but it had been slow to develop in social care/work/educational practice. Cameron and Moss (2011b) attribute this, in part, to language and cultural differences and that many of the concepts used in social pedagogy do not have a direct English translation. Another impact could also be the impact of neoliberal ideas around individualism and personal responsibility on social work practice and the influence on having a deficit-based and case management approach to working with children and their families (Smith and Whyte, 2008, cited in Cameron and Moss, 2011b). As previously mentioned, social work has changed and become much more focused on risk management and fixing problems. This is in direct contrast to the key principles of social pedagogy, which views education in its broadest sense (Petrie, 2006) and is:

> ... a perspective, including social action, which aims to promote human welfare through child-rearing and educational practices; and to prevent or ease social problems by providing people with the means to manage their own lives, and make changes in their circumstances. (Smith, 2008, p. 5, cited in Hatton, 2013, p. 12)

In the mid-2000s, New Labour began to recognise that children's care services and, in particular, residential children's homes were costly and frequently offered very little positive impact on the outcomes for the children and young people living in them. Looked after children have historically underperformed at school, are overrepresented in the criminal justice system and prison population and have poorer emotion and physical well-being than the rest of their peers (Thomas, 2005). The political motivation to construct new ways of developing children's social work/care practice began to take shape. Consecutive governments since then have continued to change the direction of social work practice and, arguably, have used the ideology of austerity to reshape children's care services. Reduction in funding for welfare services has forced children's services to think of ways to provide services that are cost effective but that also can provide good outcomes for the children using them. At the same time, the social work profession has begun to recognise its loss of direction and purpose, sensing a need to reconnect with the important core value base of social justice, dignity and worth of the person, importance of human relationships and social competence (NASW, 2011), laying the ground for social pedagogy to begin to take a foothold in social work practice.

Against this political backdrop, over the last 10 years there have been some real developments in embedding social pedagogical practice into children and young people's services. This has been influenced and directed by the ongoing work of Professor Pat Petrie, Professor Claire Cameron and the work of the Thomas Coram Research Unit (TCRU), building on their cross-national work within Europe. Their research has consistently highlighted the multiple benefits of using social pedagogical practice. The research demonstrates how social pedagogy approaches within residential children's homes can bring significant benefits, including higher numbers of young people staying in education and finding employment, less teenage pregnancy and less criminal activity (Cameron and Moss, 2011b). The benefits did not just stop at the children, the staff also gained through less staff turnover, staff feeling more connected and committed to their job, receiving more relevant training, and more importantly they felt they had the skills and knowledge to resolve issues and problems themselves (Cameron and Moss, 2011b). As a result, in 2008, the government funded a pilot programme based in children's residential units.

The aim of the children's residential pilot project was to improve the practice of staff working in residential children's homes and the outcomes for the looked after children living there as set out in the White Paper *Care Matters* (Department for Education and Skills, 2007). The aim was to take European qualified social pedagogues and employ them to work alongside residential workers with the aim of 'influencing practice from the inside and from the bottom up' (Cameron and Moss, 2011b, p. 16). Due to a lack of higher education training focused on social pedagogy at that time, it was hoped that the social pedagogues would help change practice, offer training, share practical activities based on social pedagogical ways of working but also encourage long-term sustainability of social pedagogical practice with the residential children's workers. This programme was evaluated in 2011 reporting mixed findings, partly due to the complex and difficult nature of working within residential children's homes and the British bureaucratic care system. Many of the social pedagogues identified that one of the main issues that had arisen was the cultural differences with regard to the idea of how we care for children. They felt that the English system was very paternalistic and did not see children as rich, competent beings. The social pedagogues highlighted the managerial, hierarchical and bureaucratic way staff work in comparison to the way they were used to working and the negative impact this had on their ability to care for the children. There were also issues with some residential staff not readily accepting having social pedagogues working alongside them. During the evaluation some of the residential staff explained that this was down to the social pedagogues' higher level of qualifications, which in turn meant they had more knowledge and what was seen as better practice. All of which, Cameron et al. (2011, p. 9) stated, led to a 'mismatch with the existing workforce, including their pay and conditions' and did not always lead to a harmonious relationship between residential staff and the social pedagogues.

However, even with the various challenges identified above, the overall evaluation of this project was very positive and stated that social pedagogical practice enhanced children's experience of living in residential units. The project enabled staff to engage in discussions around positive ways of caring for the children and young people they were looking after. The social pedagogues helped staff to understand the behaviour and ideas behind children's behaviour; they encouraged staff to develop reflective practice, which was then used to inform their ongoing work with the children and young people. Finally staff began to appreciate the value of their professional role and felt equal to other professionals such as social workers (Cameron et al., 2011). On a more practical level, some of the residential staff began and continued to sit and eat meals with the children and young people, creating a homely atmosphere to the residential unit. They were able to explain and link everyday tasks they were asking young people to do to their development and life skills, meaning that young people understood the point of them. Young people were encouraged to take responsibility for the running of the home and took on tasks such as planning activities, cooking and overall security of the home. Likewise, creative activities run by the social pedagogues gave staff and the young people an opportunity to understand the importance of shared experiences, doing things *with* rather than *for* the young people, as described in the *Common Third* (see Chapter 3).

Once completed, the pilot project reported that 10 out of the 18 residential units involved reported positive change as a result (Cameron et al., 2011) and it helped to secure a social pedagogical base within residential children's homes here in England. The Heartwood Care Group and St Christopher's Fellowship, amongst other organisations, have also built on the foundations of the pilot project and began developing social pedagogy within their residential children's homes. St Christopher's Fellowship have extended this approach beyond residential homes and have been growing their use of social pedagogical practice by training all of their staff and more recently their foster carers. They use a Head, Heart and Hands approach to practice and here they explain how:

1   Head

We use theory and evidence to learn and develop alongside our young people.

This is especially apparent through our pioneering work on attachment with the Centre for Abuse and Trauma Studies (CATS) at Middlesex University.

2   Heart

We use our emotional intelligence and relational skills in our reflective practice to help us develop relationships with young people, their families and our colleagues.

3   Hands

We use creative, practical activities to empower young people to learn, develop and heal from previous trauma.

(St Christopher's Fellowship, 2017)

Another major development in children's services has also been the *Head, Heart and Hands* (HHH) project run by the Fostering Network, a national organisation providing foster placements for children throughout the UK. The aim of the HHH project was to:

> … develop a social pedagogic approach within UK foster care, thereby increasing the numbers of young people in foster care who achieve their potential and make a positive contribution to society. (McDermid et al., 2016, p. 3)

The national project aimed to:

- Develop a professional, confident group of foster carers who will be able to demonstrate that by using a social pedagogic approach, they will develop the capacity to significantly improve the day to day lives of the children in their care.
- Develop social pedagogic characteristics in foster carers. Foster carers will have an integration of 'head, hands and heart' to develop strong relationships with the children they look after.
- Implement systemic change and a cultural shift which will support social pedagogic practice and recognise the central role of foster carers in shaping the lives of children within their care.
- Provide a platform for transformation of the role that foster carers play as part of the child's network.

(The Fostering Network, 2011)

Seven foster care projects were involved in the HHH project and these were spread across the UK with three in Scotland and four in England. The foster care projects, supported by social pedagogues, ran training and development sessions for foster carers focusing on explaining social pedagogy, philosophy, theory and concepts and how these could be used in their everyday care for their foster children. They offered regular refresher and support sessions to help foster carers discuss and reflect on how they were using social pedagogy and explore problems or issues with regard to their foster children. The HHH project also looked at how social pedagogy could be used to develop policies and procedures within the organisation so that they also support the aim of helping foster children reach their potential. There was also ongoing support from the Social Pedagogy Consortium, which was made up of people from Jacaranda and ThemPra and Professor Pat Petrie (McDermid et al., 2016).

The evaluation of the HHH project identified that around a third of the foster carers believed that Head, Heart, Hands had empowered and encouraged them to express warmth, respect and genuine affection for the young person (McDermid et al., 2016, p. 5). Of the other foster carers, they identified that the project had reminded them of how important a caring relationship is and the need to spend time building such a relationship, whilst '[giving] them theoretical and practical tools to do so' (McDermid et al., 2016, p. 5). These included the importance of life world orientation in understanding how a foster child may view or react to a situation because of their understanding of the world around them. In addition the Three Ps (see Chapter 3) framework they used helped them to understand and develop boundaries with their foster children, whilst also being genuinely caring and loving. Overall, the HHH project positively impacted on how the foster carers provided care and as with the children's residential staff, they felt much more confident in expressing their opinions and felt equally valued by other professionals, which improved their relationships with children's social workers. The Fostering Network have concluded that social pedagogy gives an 'ethical and theoretical framework which enhances and builds on existing practice' (The Fostering Network, 2017) and which supports foster carers to understand and develop their care for their foster children. For more information on this project see the further reading section at the end of the chapter.

As well as the two national projects mentioned above, there have also been lots of other developments within children's services. Since 2007, ThemPra and Jacaranda have been working with local authorities, including Essex, Lancashire, Staffordshire and Walsall, to support them in using social pedagogy to make changes in how children's residential services are run as well as training staff and supporting them to maintain social pedagogical practice. This has led to lots of exciting work, including Derbyshire County Council deciding to use social pedagogy as a framework to underpin all of the work they do with children who are *looked after*. This has meant that all of the staff within children's services in Derbyshire Council have received training around social pedagogy and how this can be applied to improve their practice.

But it is not only children's social services that have been embedding social pedagogy in their practice; this has also begun to spread into educational services and the London Borough of Hackney has employed social pedagogues to help them run their virtual schools service. It has long been acknowledged that *looked after* children underperform in school, leaving with little or no qualifications and very few go on to further education and university. Hackney is one of the poorest areas in England and yet via the virtual school scheme they have seen a huge improvement in the GCSE results of their *looked after* children (Cameron, 2017). Nick Corker, the virtual head teacher, attributes this to using social pedagogy to build 'good, purposeful and meaningful relationship and imaginative solutions' (Cameron, 2017). This has included using poetry workshops, creative art/music sessions and trips to interesting places and city walks, amongst other creative activities, to engage looked after children in their own education.

As discussed in Chapter 3, creativity is a significant aspect of social pedagogical practice and again there have been developments in children's services using creativity and the arts in direct work with children and young people. All local authorities have virtual schools for looked after children. Creative mentors are part of this in Derbyshire. This involves using the Pupil Premium to employ a creative professional to become a creative mentor and to run sessions with looked after children either at home, at school or in the community. Creative activities have included 'film, drama, music, poetry, photography and stories' (Derbyshire County Council, 2017). The creative mentors have used the Danish concept of the Common Third (ThemPra, 2017c) to underpin and guide their work (Figure 4.1).

Figure 4.1

The Common Third

(ThemPra, 2017c,
reproduced with the kind
permission of ThemPra)

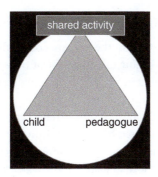

This concept has helped them develop a framework whereby the creative mentors get involved in new activities and learn alongside the children and young people they are supporting. The use of this concept has meant that the relationships with the creative mentor have been much stronger and in turn saw the mentors being able to support the looked after children to 'help them safely explore the world around them, learn new skills, communicate and address personal and emotional issues from an artistic distance' (Derbyshire County Council, 2017). A review of the service in 2016 by Dr Paul Kelly found that creative mentors had helped children to 'improve their behaviour, skills development and re-engagement in education through an increased enthusiasm, motivation and confidence' (Kelly, 2016, p. 15).

The creative mentors have also been using the Artist Pedagogue Framework developed by Professor Pat Petrie and Helen Chambers. This framework demonstrates the importance of creativity when working with children and young people and how it can support positive change. It is an outline for people to think about the principles of creativity working and how they can be applied in practice. Another good example of a creative social pedagogical project with children and young people is the Loud and Clear project run by Sage Gateshead. This is a music project aimed at working with foster and adoptive families and their children to support communication, language, physical, emotional and social development. Music sessions were held and the evaluation of the project showed that not only had the children's physical, social and emotional well-being improved, so had that of their adoptive and foster parents. They could recognise the real benefits of using music to help a child's development, support relationships and attachment as well as meeting other people who were caring for foster or adopted children. The impact, however, extended beyond the children and their families, like the creative mentors, the musicians involved in the project have said that it gave them a greater understanding of the different needs of children and an increased sense of well-being. For the social workers supporting families, they also recognised the importance of music in supporting child development but also managing challenging behaviours.

Future Areas for Development

This chapter has so far covered some of the key areas of children, young people and families social work practice that have begun to embed social pedagogy within their projects and organisations. There are many potential benefits to applying this approach in other areas of practice and for this final part of the chapter there will be a critical discussion of how social pedagogy could be applied to the youth justice system here in England. As discussed earlier, social pedagogical principles were used to build the Scottish Children's Hearings System. The English system, however, is underpinned by very different ideas and focuses on the accountability for crime, punishment and formal justice at the expense of the reduction of welfare-led approaches (Hazel, 2008, p. 6). Before looking at how social pedagogy could support positive practice within this area of children and young people's social work, there needs to be a brief explanation of the ideology, legislation and the direct working practice undertaken by Youth Offending Team (YOT) workers.

When exploring the issue of youth crime and the systemic responses to it, there are three dominant discourses that have shaped the way youth crime is seen and responded to. These are explained as punishment, welfare and treatment (Rutherford, 1992, p. 29) and the majority of youth justice systems around the world are based on one of these principles. It is important to understand what each of these principles implies and their direct influence on the way youth justice systems have developed.

A punitive approach regards crime as a rational choice that each child or young person makes, fully understanding the outcomes and consequences of their actions, which in turn means that these children and young people are then able to be held accountable for their actions. Specific punishments are linked to crimes and are viewed as valid responses to criminal behaviour. This allows society to express disapproval and see that there is proportionality between the seriousness of the crime and the punishment (Cavadino et al., 2006; Rutherford, 1992). The idea of *just deserts* is a key principle within a youth justice system based on this discourse. However it can be argued that this discourse is problematic as it disregards the universally acknowledged facts around children and young people's cognitive and emotional development.

In contrast, a system built on the welfare approach considers all children and young people who commit crime as a by-product of their environment. The child or young person's upbringing, lived experiences and lack of appropriate parenting and guidance are often seen as the reason why they have become involved in criminal behaviour, and deprivation, neglect and disadvantage are identified as key factors. With regard to dealing with criminal behaviour, this approach believes if the deprivation is dealt with then the offending will stop; so by dealing with poverty and disadvantage the children and young people will no longer commit crime (Rutherford, 1992). Again this approach is not without difficulties and often lays the blame with parents and ignores the fact that the vast majority of children grow out of criminal behaviour. It also has a *net widening* effect that formally drags children, young people and their families into official social work systems, which are then very difficult to get out of.

Once a professional is assessing and supervising a family they often see behaviour that is of a concern and due to the requirements to reduce risk and safeguard children, take a risk averse approach influenced by the *rule of pessimism* (Kettle and Jackson, 2017).

Alongside the punitive and welfare approaches there has also been a rise in the treatment approach towards the criminality of children (Cavadino et al., 2006). This approach views criminal behaviour as the consequence of a pathological condition that can be treated and cured, often with medication or psychiatric or therapeutic treatment. Assessments of individual children and young people's needs are taken into account and so treatments vary. However, this approach has been criticised for ignoring environmental and societal factors; again it lays the blame at the feet of the individual and takes a medical standpoint in believing that treatment is the answer (Rutherford, 1992). It also tends to be quite punitive in nature as children and young people's behaviour is seen as problematic and in need of rectifying.

The English youth justice system is very firmly set within the punitive discourse around crime and punishment. As Wyness (2006) details, there has been 'an inflated political "arms race" over many years. In an attempt to sound more punitive, politicians have made piece-meal changes to the youth justice system.' This has been to the detriment of the needs of the child involved in the youth justice system (Wyness, 2006). Instead, there have been negative discourses around guilt, responsibility and punishment at the heart of the modern English youth justice system. Over the last 20 years there has been a dramatic shift in English youth justice policy that has seen the welfare of the child pushed aside to be replaced with the punishment and accountability of children for their actions (Cavadino and Dignan, 2006; Scott and Codd, 2010). One high profile criminal case caused public outrage after high levels of negative media attention, and solidified the punitive approach of the English youth justice system. This was the case of John Thompson and Robert Venables who were charged and found guilty of the murder of James Bulger. This case and the ensuing public outcry led directly to a tougher government stance on youth crime. This was a violent and terrible crime, yet it is worth remembering that there have only been 27 similar cases in the last 150 years, where children have murdered another child. Yet this case shaped the direction of youth justice policy and government rhetoric which is still being felt today.

This punitive stance can be seen in practice when viewing government legislation such as the Crime and Disorder Act (CDA) (1998). This piece of legislation saw all youth justice services moved from the Children's Services Department to the direct remit of the Home Office. This government department oversees everything to do with crime, policing, immigration, drugs policy and anti-terrorism. So this departmental shift highlighted the political ideology around the changing focus in response to youth crime by the government at that time. The CDA (1998) also removed the notion of *doli incapax*, a legal principle that had stood for hundreds of years and stated that children up until the age of 14 could not be presumed to fully understand the consequences of their actions (Frost and Parton, 2009; Smith, 2012). After the implementation of this Act, many commentators stated that England had the most draconian system of juvenile justice in Europe (Cavadino et al., 2006; Goldson and Muncie, 2011). Goldson and Muncie (2011) ascertained that this has led directly to the *adultification* of children and young people and the belief that they act with full intention and capacity and should be treated like adults. Another impact of this punitive approach is that as the prosecution no longer has to prove the criminal intent of a child or young person, more cases against children have now been brought before courts and we have one of the largest youth justice systems in Europe.

Another problematic area within our youth justice system is around the age that a child or young person can be charged with committing an offence, known legally as the age of criminal responsibility. The European Social Rights Committee has been very critical about the age limit set here in England as we have the lowest of any European country. They stated that the age of criminal responsibility should be raised from 10 to 14 years old, in line with other EU countries and reflecting the UNCRC (1989: Article 4) and the protection of children's rights. In countries that have higher ages of criminal responsibility, such as Norway, set at 14 years old, and Belgium, which has it set at 18 years old, there are very low levels of crime. This demonstrates that there is no link between the age of criminal responsibility and young people committing crime, which is one that is often used against raising it here in England. But this is an issue, as when we look at other aspects of children and young people's lives there are lots of pieces of legislation that clearly limit what they can do due to their age. For example, they cannot get married till they are 16 years old, they cannot buy alcohol or cigarettes till they are 18 years old and under the Pet Animals Act (1951) children under 12 years old cannot buy a pet. They can be tried for a criminal offence from 10 years old but not deemed responsible enough to purchase a rabbit or goldfish.

The CDA (1998) set out that:

> It shall be the principal aim of [the] youth justice system to prevent offending by children and young people. (S.37 CDA 1998) and that every Local Authority must do everything *reasonably possible to prevent crime and disorder in its area.* (CDA 1998)

To meet this aim the Act also laid out the legal framework for the Youth Offending Teams (YOT) and set about standardising the assessments, court reports and sentencing options for children and young people. Using the YOT assessment, or ASSET document as it is known, I plan to offer a critical discussion about how the implementation of social pedagogy could be used to positive effect within the youth justice system.

> Asset provides a common, structured framework for assessment of all young people involved in the criminal justice system. It is a standard assessment of the factors contributing to a young person's offending. Research commissioned by the Youth Justice Board has established the main risk factors that lead to youth offending and also the protective factors that can prevent it. (Youth Justice Board, 2014)

There have been concerns about the effectiveness of this standardised assessment and the reliance on the identified risk factors to predict future reoffending. This has also been to the detriment of YOT officers using their own analytical and assessment skills as part of ASSET and leading them to focus on gaining information required by the system instead of understanding offending from the child or young person's perspective. Because of these concerns the assessment has been updated and the new ASSET Plus developed, which has also been linked to evidence-based practice and research. The main focus of ASSET Plus is on strong assessments that focus on risk and the protective factors in a child and young person's life. However the major change and link to social pedagogy is in that YOT officers now have to gain a understanding of how a young person views their life/behaviour, a clear link to the concept of Life World Orientation. Other key factors contained in the focus of the new ASSET Plus and social pedagogical theories and concepts are shown in Table 4.1.

Table 4.1 ASSET Plus and Social Pedagogy (ThemPra, 2018)

Key Focus of ASSET Plus Assessments	Social Pedagogy Theory/Concept
Understanding young people's behaviour. Using context, situation and perceptions by the young person.	Life World Orientation: Helps the YOT officer understand the 'lived world' and the child or young person's daily/weekly routines and the pragmatic strategies they may have developed to cope with difficult situations. The four dimensions used within this concept are: Time, Space, Social Relations and Cultural Interpretations.
Understanding and working with risk. Risk needs to be balanced with needs/positive development.	Risk Competence: This approach supports the child or young person in learning about potential dangers and developing strategies to manage those dangers rather than be absolutely protected from them in advance. Eichsteller and Holthoff (2009) refer to the term *risk competence* to describe the process whereby children become more knowledgeable and skilled in assessing risks and therefore acquire the competence to take risks more safely.
Identifying strengths. These need to be explained and contextualized by the young person.	Diamond Model: The fours aspects of Well-Being and Happiness, Holistic Learning, Relationships and Empowerment can be used as a framework to identify strengths in a child and young person's life.
Desistance and willingness to change.	Zone of Proximal Development: This theory contains four steps in supporting positive change: *Starting from the child's motivation to learn*

(Continued)

Table 4.1 (Continued)

Key Focus of ASSET Plus Assessments	Social Pedagogy Theory/Concept
A clear understanding of how the young person views change.	Children want to learn and are interested in finding out new things – this provides a great opportunity for social pedagogues to support their learning.
	Starting from where the pedagogue thinks the child 'is'
	The starting point for learning is where the child is at, and the social pedagogue can assess this through observations, reflection and dialogue.
	Mutual process of learning together, e.g. Common Third
	Learning can also be a mutual process, in which both the social pedagogue and the child learn something new and support each other in this.
	Necessary development, things that need to be learned
	(Schwartz, 2001, cited in ThemPra, 2018)
Involvement of young people and their families.	Relational Universe:
	This concept acknowledges the importance of relationships, positive or negative, in a child or young person's life. It supports a YOT officer to gain an understanding of who is in the 'relational universe' of that child or young person and the impact and influence it has on their lives.
	It recognizes the importance of interdependency that we all have as human beings instead of focusing on independence. The Relational Universe uses mutual support and reciprocity to help develop a strong and reliable social network in a vast number of social settings.

Conclusion

Throughout this chapter I have focused on some of the large-scale social pedagogy projects that have happened over the last 10 years or so and identified a possible area of growth. Even though social pedagogy is still heavily linked to residential and children's foster care, it has begun to move out into other fields of practice within children and young people's services. Through the work of professionals who want to reclaim the 'heart' within social work, and supported by ThemPra, Jacaranda, the Thomas Coram Research Unit, the Social Pedagogue Development Network and the Social Pedagogy Professional Association (SPPA), it continues to grow and develop.

Further Reading

Head, Heart and Hands, Fostering Network:

www.thefosteringnetwork.org.uk/policy-practice/projects-and-programmes/head-heart-
    hands

Creative Mentors, Derbyshire County Council:

www.local.gov.uk/derbyshire-county-council-using-creative-mentoring-support-looked-
    after-children

Knowledge and skills for children and family social work:

https://assets.publishing.service.gov.uk/government/uploads/system/uploads/
    attachment_data/file/338718/140730_Knowledge_and_skills_statement_final_version_
    AS_RH_Checked.pdf

ADOPTING SOCIAL PEDAGOGICAL APPROACHES IN WORKING WITH ADULTS

ALI GARDNER

It is true to say that much of the literature and examples of practice around social pedagogy relate to work with children and young people. In this chapter, I aim to explore how social pedagogy provides a useful framework for working alongside adults receiving social care. In so doing, I will demonstrate how social pedagogy can enhance the role of those involved with delivering social work and social care. Finally, the chapter will consider the compatibility of social pedagogy within the current legislative, policy and economic context.

Social Pedagogy – Key Concepts

In order to explore the relevance of social pedagogy in our work with adults, it may be useful to consider some of the key social pedagogical concepts discussed earlier in this book as this supports the application of theory into practice.

Haltung

Social pedagogy recognises that our values are of central importance in working alongside individuals and communities. This is referred to as *Haltung*, a German word roughly translating as ethos, mindset or attitude. In Chapter 3 this concept was explored in some depth. We will now begin to explore why this concept is relevant and how it can be applied in practice to working alongside adults who access social care. Working with adults requires both a personal and political engagement with our values. At a personal level it requires an absolute commitment to respecting the uniqueness and potential of each individual. At a political level it requires an understanding of the relationship between individuals who use services and the state itself. For example, disabled people, for many years, have challenged the paternalistic nature of welfare delivery, demanding their right to be treated as equal active citizens (Morris, 2004). This is no easy task for social workers, who generally work in organisations that have a long history of deeply embedded paternalistic values shaping practice. In order to adopt a social pedagogical approach to their work, social workers may need to examine their relationships with service users and realign their values, skills and practice in viewing people as experts in their own right rather than passive recipients of care (Gardner, 2014). Similarly, Smale et al. (1993) suggest that changing practice requires workers to change the assumptions they make about individuals. Wieninger (2000) points out that our *Haltung* influences how we think about others and the notions we hold about who they are. The fundamental nature of *Haltung* means that every engagement must be authentic and based on an emotional connectedness to people with a profound respect for their human dignity. This therefore requires both an intellectual (head) and emotional (heart) engagement with our interactions with individuals and communities. It is important to note here that social pedagogy is equally concerned with society as it is with the pedagogical relationship we enter with individuals. Coussée et al. (2010) warn of the danger of isolating pedagogical action from social context. A lack of critical reflection on the broader political, economic and cultural conditions shaping society runs the risk of social work being reduced to a solution-orientated approach whereby expert professionals seek individualised strategies to cure social problems (Coussée et al., 2010). Importantly, social work needs to continually seek out the role it can play in this space between the individual and society whilst promoting self-efficacy and learning as a means to achieve this.

This explains why social pedagogy is more concerned with *how* something is done rather than *what* is done (Hämäläinen, 2003). At this point it would seem logical to link the concept of Head, Heart and Hands to our work with adults. Swiss social reformer and educator Pestalozzi (1746–1827) coined the term *Head, Heart and Hands*. He asserted the inseparable nature of all three. In relation to our work with adults, we continually need to identify, connect and share knowledge and learn from one another using our heads. This will require an understanding of academic knowledge, research and theory. The heart ensures that we maintain an emotional connectedness with individuals and regard for them at all times. Finally the hands symbolise the importance of the practical application of our engagements with individuals. The hands represent us acting as a consequence of processes, knowledge and information. In working alongside adults, this is likely to involve enabling adults to undertake the practical tasks which 'promote their inclusion, participation, social identity and social competence as a member of society' (Hämäläinen, 2003, p. 76). Central to this concept is the notion of advocacy and the ability to adopt facilitative rather than instructive roles in supporting adults.

The Diamond Model

As we discussed in Chapter 3, the Diamond Model (Eichsteller and Holthoff, 2012), outlines the most central principles guiding social pedagogy. Human beings are precious and have rich knowledge, skills and abilities. Centrally, this model encourages a strengths-based approach when working alongside individuals and communities. Recognising the strengths and gifts rather than deficits or problems is key to all our engagements. For social workers, this is reflected in a social model approach (Oliver, 2009) whereby disability is understood, essentially, as a result of the way society is organised rather than as an inability of the individual. A commitment to this stance is important. If we believe that our *Haltung* influences our practice, we must accept, therefore, that our understanding of disability will inform our conceptualisation of the professional task. This in itself is a huge cultural shift for social workers who have traditionally been trained to use their professionalism to assess need against prescribed criteria, thus inadvertently promoting the adoption of the medical model, which tends to focus on limitations of the individuals (Crow, 1995, cited in Barnes and Mercer, 2010). Crucially, social pedagogues must adopt dynamic, critical, integrative and creative approaches to their work, as suggested by Coussée et al. (2010), rather than mechanical, procedural and automated responses.

Well-being and happiness

The Diamond Model promotes the need to address well-being and happiness. In social pedagogical terms, the focus needs to be on sustainability rather than meeting short-term needs. It is interesting to note that well-being has been recognised within the law and is the leading principle of the Care Act (2014). The statutory guidance states the importance of recognising a person as best placed to judge their own well-being. The inclusion of individuals' wishes, views, feelings and beliefs to promote inclusion and participation is clearly articulated with this Act along with an insistence that well-being must be at the 'heart of all care support' (DoH, 2018). Again this presents a significant shift for social workers, who have traditionally focused on the professional task of assessment and arranging the provision of support to adults with care needs, under previous legislation and policy. Although seemingly subtle, Hatton (2013) points out the significance of a shifting narrative from welfare to well-being. The latter represents a very different engagement with the state, reflecting the participatory role of the individual as opposed to the state delivering welfare within a paternalistic model of care. Later in the chapter we will consider some of the challenges in promoting well-being within the current political and economic climate. Nevertheless, the notion of well-being as it is expressed within the legislation and statutory guidance reflects social pedagogical thinking and potentially, therefore, provides opportunities for social workers to engage with new narratives and approaches in their work. The good news for social workers is that there is a wealth of knowledge, literature, research and experience to draw upon in finding practical ways of promoting well-being. The development of person-centred practice by supporters such as Helen Sanderson who described 'a process of continual listening, and learning: focused on what is important to someone now, and for the future' (Sanderson, 2000, p. 2) has enhanced our understanding of well-being along with the practical tools to deliver this in practice, and reflects social pedagogical approaches to our work.

Holistic learning

Of all the concepts presented within the social pedagogical discipline, learning is perhaps a more slippery concept to grasp within an adult context. It is often assumed that learning is something we do as a child and less relevant to adult life unless we engage in formal education. Social pedagogy, however, stresses the centrality of learning in working alongside individuals. Recognising the potential for growth and a better understanding of oneself is key to promoting and achieving well-being, and according to German philosopher Sloterdijk (cited in Kahl, 2001, p. 110), 'Learning is the pleasant anticipation of oneself.' Social pedagogy recognises the importance of life-long learning in supporting the acquisition of new skills, the promotion of confidence and developing a sense of purpose as individuals adjust, adapt and embrace challenges, opportunities and transitions along the life course. Just as a child learns new skills for each stage of their development, as adults we continue to face changes, some of which we expect and others that we do not: for instance a loss in mobility linked to age or illness or the sudden death of a partner, both of which would require the need to adapt and learn new skills. As adults we may draw on earlier experiences and learning to guide us through new transitions, whilst, at the same time, we continue to learn and develop new strategies at each stage or life event. Anderson (2008) stresses the importance of learning in later life in order to enhance older people's capacity to exercise choice and determine their circumstances. Likewise, Hafford-Letchfield (2010) notes the transformative potential of learning for older people, allowing for a more meaningful engagement with concepts such as social capital and genuine co-production, thus enabling individuals to take an active role in improving and sustaining their well-being. At a practical level this might involve learning to manage or direct one's own care and support, management of emerging health issues, changing mental capacity and the meaningfulness of life. For many individuals this may well require the involvement and support of others, but the opportunity to learn provides an ideal vehicle to exercise autonomy rather than a more traditional model of *managed care* whereby the expert professional directs care and support. Hafford-Letchfield (2010) suggests life-long learning seeks to promote *active ageing* rather than a *burden of ageing*.

As social workers, therefore, we need to consider the role we can play in supporting the learning process. Creating an environment conducive to learning urges us to consider notions of power, expertise and partnerships. As we have discussed earlier, social work engagements, traditionally, have been based upon professionals using their professional expertise to assess needs and to make professional recommendations. It may therefore be necessary to revisit such previous assumptions and find new ways of engagement that promote a more equal approach to the professional task. The belief that the professional and the individual can learn together requires social workers to reshape their roles as enablers, facilitators and community connectors (Gardner, 2014). This requires more than simply signposting individuals to relevant support services. We will explore the benefits of learning further when we discuss the Learning Zone and the Common Third.

Relationships

As discussed in Chapter 1, social pedagogy insists upon the importance of relationships, based on empathy, warmth and genuineness on the part of the worker, as described by Carl Rogers in 1951 (Rogers, 1995). Whilst it is no surprise to social workers that relationships are a key resource, the profession has continued to struggle with our actual application in practice. Howe (1998) reported social workers becoming confused and ambivalent in regard to the importance of relationships. Understanding the professional nature of the relationship and the need to understand professional boundaries has continued to be a frequently visited debate over the last 20 years. In their research with adults, Beresford and Andrews (2012) found that service users reported, above everything else, the importance of the relationship they had with their social worker and stated that it provided a crucial starting point for getting help and support on equal terms. The inseparable nature of the internal and external worlds of individuals has been well documented in relationship-based practice in social work (see Ruch, 2005; Trevithick, 2003). Both emphasise the use of self and the relationship as an integral component of any professional intervention. The Three Ps model discussed in Chapter 3 addresses the issue of boundaries and professionalism within relationships. In order to become an effective social pedagogue, one must utilise both the professional and personal aspects of oneself. The key challenge therefore is achieving the right balance and recognising when and how the inclusion of the *personal* is purposeful and supporting the engagement with the individual. One has to be authentic and become skilled at making positive use of one's personality. Adopting this model when working alongside adults may well be different from our work with children. For example, there may be more or different opportunities to relate as an adult to another adult and sharing personal experience in an appropriate manner may support the building of the relationship and help to achieve desired outcomes. The Three Ps are constantly in play when we work alongside individuals and whilst the fluidity of this framework is its key strength, it can also be a potential danger. Practitioners need to employ careful and constant reflection to ensure they are making appropriate use of each strand.

Empowerment

An inherent commitment to empowerment should underpin all our work with adults. The problem with the word empowerment is that it is often used too casually to describe activities that describe singular events or exchanges in which social workers believe they have empowered a service user by supporting them to undertake an activity or take control of a challenging situation. Whilst this positive experience may well contribute towards the person regaining control in their day-to-day living and start to build capacity, it is unlikely to make long-lasting changes unless the individuals can reflect on their own experiences of disempowerment. This will involve understanding the connections between their own circumstances and the broader socio-political context in which they exist. As discussed earlier in the chapter, Coussée et al. (2010) stress the importance of connecting the individual and society, or pedagogical action and social context. This calls upon an important learning process between the professional and the individual whereby both can examine and support one another in understanding the significance of disadvantage and oppression that individuals face in everyday life. A key element of social pedagogy is the focus on the person as a whole, who is influenced by, and influences, the environment around them (Hatton, 2013). The need to therefore connect the personal with the political becomes imperative as individuals can use this insight to motivate themselves to make decisions and changes that are likely to have a long-lasting effect. Gardner (2014, p. 38) suggests that the belief of the necessity to take an action becomes more important than the ability to take the action as the individual develops an internal compass that can navigate them through complex decisions and situations. One key misconception of empowerment is the belief that independence is the ultimate aim. For many, the concept and ideology behind independence have been unhelpful in social care. Brisenden (1986) and Morris (2004) suggest that disabled people have become *victims of ideology* as the notion of independence has been defined and understood as being able to do things such as dressing, washing and cooking for oneself. The Independent Living Movement asserted that independence should be defined simply by being able to achieve one's goals. However, this first definition of independence remains the stated goal in much of the work social and health care practitioners are involved in, particularly with adults.

For some disabled adults and older people, there is a danger that many of their daily engagements involve paid professionals in situations where they are receiving some form of support. The opportunities therefore to contribute to the relationship or *bring something to the table* are limited. The act of reciprocity has long been documented as an essential part of forming a meaningful relationship (Blyth and Gardner, 2007; Williams, 1995). The opportunity to engage in reciprocal relationships whereby social exchange operates bringing equity to interdependent relationships is key to empowerment. Interestingly, the Care Act (2014) has explicitly recognised the importance of one's ability to 'contribute' as one of the nine domains of well-being in Section 1 of the legislation.

Social pedagogy insists upon emphasising the notions of both independence and interdependence. Eichsteller and Holthoff (2012) suggest that as humans we are intricately connected. As human beings we are constantly dependent on others. Importantly, interdependence conveys the reciprocal nature of this relationship, suggesting that as humans we give and receive support in a variety of ways. If we accept that positive relationships are central to one's well-being, we must support the formation and maintenance of meaningful relationships for individuals in their own lives.

At this point, we must return once again to the relationship between the individual and society/community. In order to bring some practical application to notions of interdependency it might be useful to consider Rothuizen and Harbo's (2017) concept of *meaningful belonging*. Stressing the importance of interdependency of social inclusion and community development on the one hand, and individual rights and well-being on the other, Rothuizen and Harbo suggest that the role of the pedagogue is to create situations in which the other person can act meaningfully, through the process of 'bonding and bridging' (p. 17).

In order to do this, the pedagogue must be part of that relationship and needs to become part of the other person's everyday life. Rothuizen and Harbo (2017) suggest that the practitioner needs to enter into an inclusive relationship whereby the pedagogical task focuses on building self-confidence, self-respect and self-esteem, which are reinforced by a sense of belonging and participation (*bonding*). In turn this increased self-belief can lead towards trying out other activities and groups in society (*bridging*) whereby the individual moves towards being part of an inclusive community. It is interesting to note that the narrative underpinning current legislation and policy is one of building strengths-based and assets-based approaches to adult social care. The focus of *inclusive community* is very much a part of this language. Likewise, research continues to confirm the inextricable links between ageing well and domains of community and associational life (Russell, 2011). Social work, however, often takes place through outcomes-driven processes with limited attention to the value of the relationship between the practitioner and individual in achieving outcomes. Social pedagogy asserts the focal point of relationships, recognising the power it can play in supporting individuals to achieve meaningful, sustainable outcomes whereby they feel connected to their communities.

Positive experiences

Social pedagogy promotes a dynamic, creative approach to working alongside individuals. In order to engage individuals in this process, there is a benefit in them experiencing positive experiences. We have already discussed the benefit of employing a strengths-based approach to our work that is fundamentally based upon the belief that all individuals have abilities and gifts (Graybeal, 2001). Through recognising and valuing the power of experiencing something positive, the professional can play a key role in capitalising on this initial experience of positivity and exploring how this can be internalised by the individual, leading to capacity-building and a longer lasting positive impact. Trevithick (2003) considered the impact of *energizing* and *de-energizing* experiences for individuals. In her analysis, she explored how negative experiences often led to defensive responses triggered to protect oneself. The energy required to struggle to survive and cope, she suggested, led to individuals becoming blocked and immobilised, with little emotional energy left for the task of growth.

It is not an uncommon experience to work with adults who have, through no choice of their own, found themselves dependent on welfare delivery, whether as a result of a physical or learning disability, age or illness, or perhaps as a carer. Many such individuals have found themselves frustrated in navigating cumbersome, powerful organisations for many years.

This in itself can be a very de-energising experience, often with no hope of ever escaping. It is absolutely essential in working alongside individuals that professionals recognise the location of social work within a context that often contributes to individuals feeling helpless and hopeless at times and preventing them from engaging in personal growth. This could be something as simple as waiting for the response to a letter or application or being transferred to several different departments on the telephone to reach the right person. It may be the experience of continually being placed in a position where they have to focus and argue the extremes of their disability: emphasising everything they are unable to do in order to meet stringent thresholds to be eligible for support. Again social pedagogy insists upon the recognition of the person as a whole affected by their environment and the social position they are afforded by society and its structures/institutions used to deploy welfare. It is therefore crucial that this struggle is recognised for each individual. It is only then that professionals can start to identify and seek positive, appropriate energising experiences. In so doing, the individuals can be supported to experience a different use of their emotional energy, which makes capacity-building more likely.

In supporting individuals to experience positive experiences, professionals need to strike the right balance between acknowledging the real external, sometimes impenetrable, barriers that prevent growth whilst at the same time believing and committing to each individual's potential for growth. As Weick (1983, p. 133) suggests:

> We have an innate 'life force' that will strive for fundamental change based on innate
> curiosity, need for stimulation and desire for fulfillment.

Eichsteller and Holthoff (2011a) place positive experiences in the middle of the Diamond Model as they represent the means of achieving the four core aims discussed above. Enabling individuals to engage in positive experiences has the power to build self-confidence and self-worth, which in turn can reinforce happiness and well-being. The opportunity and satisfaction from learning and developing strong relationships support the individual in feeling empowered and strengthened. Many of us will recognise these core aims as a key motivation for us in entering the social work profession. It is important, however, that we continue to challenge ourselves and our organisations, to ensure that they remain at the forefront of our practice, particularly at times when structural and financial obstacles stand in our way. Using frameworks such as the Diamond Model provide a simple and useful tool to ensure that we are giving equal attention to each core aim and supporting individuals to engage in positive experiences wherever possible.

 **ACTIVITY 5.1**

The Diamond model in practice

Using the Diamond Model, think about someone you have worked alongside and map each strand to the individual. You could draw a template of the diamond as a visual aid to support you. Firstly, you should consider the four core aims of well-being and happiness, holistic learning, relationships and empowerment.

Well-being and happiness

Firstly think about what makes this person happy in their life. This could be something very simple such as having a nice cup of coffee each morning whilst doing the crossword; it could include spending time with people who are important to them or planning a trip/holiday. Next, consider the physical, intellectual, emotional and social aspects of well-being for this individual. It is important to focus on both the short-term and long-term aspects of well-being.

Holistic learning

Try and consider any aspect of learning that currently takes place for this individual. This could include things such as joining a new social group or club, learning a new skill, learning to adapt to a new stage or circumstance in their life.

Relationships

Identify important relationships in this person's life. This could include both family and friends and those who offer support in a professional role. It is important to consider both relationships that are viewed as positive and negative ones.

Empowerment

Think about the times where this person has control over decisions they make about their life. This could include daily living tasks and also more long-term plans.

Secondly, think about possible positive experiences that could support and strengthen the individual's diamond. You could carry out this exercise with the individual themselves or complete it independently. It is important that you recognise both the positive and negative impact of each strand. For example, learning may bring great joy to an individual as they develop a new skill but it could also represent a very negative challenge. Think about the positive experiences that might ease this process and motivate the individual to focus on the benefits. It will be useful to share your diamond with a colleague and discuss the different points on the diamond.

Common Third

As we discussed in Chapter 3, the Common Third is central to social pedagogical practice. Essentially it is a purposeful activity to strengthen relationships. It involves learning together and at its core promotes notions of equality and respect. Much of the literature surrounding the use of the Common Third relates to work with children. In working with adults, the Common Third offers many opportunities similar to those when working with children. Fundamentally, it recognises the quality of the relationship as a powerful resource in supporting individuals to achieve desired change. Many social work theories/methods such as task-centred practice, for example, reflect some elements of the Common Third. Marsh and Doel (2005) describe the importance of the relationship between the professional and the individual in setting and reviewing the task (the object) to aid capacity-building, self-belief and motivation for the individual (subject). The difference here is that the task belongs to the individual rather than a shared activity in which both parties are learning. Hatton (2013), however, notes the importance of a deliberate focus on the activity as something that is shared, which in principle implies equality. He also stresses the importance of both learning together, which again addresses issues of power in the relationship. Working in this way is likely to be unfamiliar to social workers working with adults as there is often an assumption by both the professional and the individual that the contribution of expertise is a key part of the professional's role. It is interesting to note the changing language in more recent policy and legislation. The statutory guidance supporting the Care Act (2014) emphasises the importance of recognising the expertise individuals bring to their own situations. The Common Third provides opportunities for individuals and professionals to enter into a relationship where they can forget the hierarchies around them and devote entirely to the process and activity. In this sense the intended outcome becomes the strengthened relationship, which, in turn, can be used effectively for personal growth, and achieving desired change. We will discuss some of the challenges to embedding this approach into current structures later in the chapter. It is interesting to note that Common Third activities were often used in traditional social work and supported living models. It was not uncommon as a social worker in the 1980s and 1990s to use activities as a vehicle to engage with service users. This type of engagement is now more likely to be viewed as a luxury in social work, suggesting that meaningful genuine relationships with service users are less important that identifying and responding to the eligible needs.

Learning Zone

Earlier in this chapter, we discussed the concept of learning as a central thread of social pedagogy. In working with adults, this requires specific consideration and application. Recogniszing learning and personal growth as inseparable concepts is probably a good starting point when engaging with individuals. For adults who have been dependent on support to enable them to meet many of their needs, there may be more challenges in daring to move outside of their comfort zone and imagine different situations or arrangements. We know that fear and negative energies can affect how people respond to challenge or change. As a social worker, I can clearly remember the fear and anxiety that gripped some adults with learning disabilities who were moving from long stay institutions to community-based living as part of the resettlement programme. The fear of taking a risk to learn and experience new ways of living outside their secure environments immobilised many individuals. Supporting this process was further complicated by the fact that the cognitive ability to understand why this was happening was limited for some individuals and consequently made this a frightening and slow process. Supporting people from the comfort zone to the learning zone without slipping into the panic zone can be a very tricky manoeuvre. Another key reflection of this work highlighted the necessity of seeing oneself (as the practitioner) as a learner. Walking into long stay institutions as a newly qualified social worker still remains one of the most powerful experiences of my practice. I found it difficult to understand this way of living that seemed so closed off from the rest of the community. I was struck by how different it was from what I had expected and I quickly realised I had a lot to learn in a short space of time in order to work effectively in supporting people through this huge transition.

From a social pedagogical perspective, the focus on shared learning is helpful in guiding both the individual and the practitioner. From an individual's perspective, Viscott (2003, p. 89) very much captures the purpose of learning:

> If you want to feel secure do what you already know how to do. But if you want to grow ...
> go to the cutting edge of your competence, which means a temporary loss of security. So,
> whenever you don't quite know *what you are doing know that you are growing ...*

From a practitioner's perspective the Learning Zone model is helpful in opening oneself to new thinking. This often involves a process of unlearning and breaking free from previous conceptualisations. This involves making conscious steps to move beyond the comfort zone into the learning zone. It may be useful to draw on early work from Turner (1987), who refers to a phase of being 'betwixt and between', a *liminal space* in which one lets go of 'what is' and moves towards 'what will be'. It is a state of suspension and ambiguity in which individuals are afforded the rare opportunity to reflect and contemplate. The *liminal space* permits an integration of new knowledge into a new way of seeing and new conceptualisations. Similarly, Perkins (2006, in Meyer and Land, 2006) suggests that it is the state of being *stuck* and *letting go* that allows other things to come into view. Social work is, undoubtedly, experiencing a period of intense formation and transformation (Ferguson and Woodward, 2009). It is clear that new ways of viewing both the way welfare is delivered and the relationship between those who access care and support and the state are needed to meet changing demands and landscapes. So for the practitioner there needs to be a willingness to continually learn. Morgan (2012) refers to *threshold concepts*, which, she believes, have five central characteristics, namely: transformative, irreversible, integrative, bounded and troublesome. She uses the example of teaching the social model of disability to illustrate the shift students make when they question preconceived ideas about disabled people being tragic, passive recipients of care in need of expert help. Through immersing themselves in new knowledge they begin to see how disability is socially constructed by society and locate the problem as being external to the individual. Morgan suggests that students need to *get it* and once they have *got it*, i.e. passed through the threshold, they develop different ways of accessing knowledge and new ways of thinking about things. In this sense the process is irreversible. It is impossible to step back to previous ways of understanding. This can be a troubling period as it can deeply affect one's whole identity and questions many assumptions that have been made along the way.

In many ways, liminal spaces and threshold concepts describe the movement from the comfort zone to the learning zone and reflect the ideas that social pedagogues such as Tom Senninger (2000, cited in ThemPra, 2017a) proposed in terms of 'living out curiosity and making new discoveries to expand'.

The relevance for social work with adults in the current climate is most pertinent given the renewed focus on strengths-based practice, the well-being concept and person-centred practice. Additionally, the challenges presented by changing demographics leading to increased levels of need at a time of austerity are forcing or opening (depending on one's perception) opportunities to think and practise in very different ways.

Social Pedagogy, Legislation and Policy

Much of the language used in current adult care legislation and policy reflects social pedagogical thinking. It is clear that the recent Care Act (2014) has deliberately promoted a narrative that insists upon the centrality of self-determined well-being, choice and control. Both in the Act itself and the supporting statutory guidance there are clear indications of a commitment to employing strengths-based and person-centred approaches to both assessment and the delivery of care and support. The Personalisation agenda has undoubtedly influenced the new language being used, as has the continued campaigning by disabled adults, older people and their carers, insisting upon support that allows them to be actively involved in designing and controlling it. Likewise, Hatton (2013) suggests that the recent focus on co-production resonates with elements of social pedagogy such as Head, Heart and Hands, notions of creativity and the Common Third. The emphasis on relationships, partnership working and the involvement of the broader community reflects social pedagogical approaches. Importantly from a social pedagogical perspective, this shared approach between the practitioner and the individual 'seeks to produce beneficial outcomes through processes of interaction and the minimization of power differentials' (Hatton, 2013, p. 78).

It is not possible, however, to ignore key demographic changes such as the increase in older people living longer with more complex conditions such as dementia and chronic illness and the future impact this will have on the provision of care and support (DoH, 2007). Likewise, we cannot ignore the impact of sweeping cuts to public services by current and previous governments. One therefore could not be criticised for questioning the motivation of policy narratives of choice, control and self-determined well-being. In responding to the Personalisation agenda, Ferguson (2012) describes personalisation as an offspring of two discourses: independent living and neoliberalism. Both share a language of independence, choice and control but emerge from very different origins. Similarly, Duffy (in Needham and Glasby, 2014) questions whether there is a genuine commitment to personalisation or whether it has become one of the means by which cuts have been introduced:

> At worst personalisation has become 'zombie' personalisation. The language and structures of self-directed support are used, but the underlying spirit is hostile to citizenship. (Duffy, in Needham and Glasby, 2014, p. 178)

Conclusion

In this chapter, we have revisited some of the concepts introduced in Chapter 3, exploring their relevance and application within an adult social care context. It is interesting to note the influence both legislation/policy and theoretical disciplines can assert on the social work role. At times this convergence can be useful in understanding the task and its practical application. Social care professionals, however, must remain mindful of the distinction between theory and legislation/policy. As Duffy, above, warns of *zombie personalisation*, there is a danger that policy makers, seeing the appeal of social pedagogy, attempt to slot it into existing structures without acknowledging the critical engagement of *head, heart* and *hands* that is required in assuming social pedagogical practice.

This quandary only serves to reinforce the premise upon which social pedagogy is based, *how* you do something is infinitely more important than *what* you do, or in fact what you name it.

Further Reading

At this point you may find it useful to refer to the Care Act Statutory Guidance and consider the principle of *well-being* and how this might relate to the social pedagogical concepts discussed above. Likewise, you should refer to the section on person-centred care and support planning and consider how concepts such as the Diamond Model and the Learning Zone might be used positively to achieve the aims set out in the Care Act (2014).

www.gov.uk/government/publications/care-act-statutory-guidance

It will also be useful to reflect on the *Knowledge and Skills Statement for Social Workers in Adult Services* (DoH, 2015b). Many of the concepts discussed in this chapter clearly link to the expectations set out in the *Knowledge and Skills Statement* including relationship-based practice, strengths-based approaches and outcome-focused support planning, all of which recognise and respect the expertise of the individual.

https://assets.publishing.service.gov.uk/government/uploads/system/uploads/attachment_data/file/411957/KSS.pdf

PARTICIPATION

LINDY SIMPSON

Introduction

What do people mean by 'participation'? It is a familiar word that seems straightforward enough, so why does it have an entire chapter dedicated to it? This chapter will explore these questions with a focus on participation in decision-making within social work and social pedagogical practice. The fact that you are interested and reading this book indicates, I hope, that you connect with the value base of taking a participatory approach and want to know more. The Social Pedagogy Professional Association Standards (SPPA, 2017) provide a useful starting point as Standard 5 identifies that the social pedagogue will, 'Enable people to use their voices and effect change within their own lives and wider society'. The social pedagogue will aim to achieve this by 'creat[ing] opportunities and contexts for people to actively participate in society, express their own views and listen to those of others'.

The Health and Care Professions Council (HCPC) Social Workers' Standards of Proficiency are written for social workers to 'understand, know' and 'be able to apply' the standards (2017, p. 17). To understand participation we need to understand our own values and through self-reflection learn how our personal values link to our practice approach. Sinclair (2004, p. 111) identified 'there is much for adults to reflect upon, from their particular perspective, if participation is to be more meaningful, effective and sustainable'. Freire (1970, p. 47) adds 'reflection – true reflection – leads to action'. It is essential that practitioners understand this dynamic process from their own position and continue to identify and make sense of conflicting approaches to participation and rights-based practice. Case studies will be used in the chapter to recognise there is a spectrum of participatory practice. The chapter will define participation, introduce key concepts and theoretical frameworks. The second part of the chapter will explore the application of participation with individuals and organisations, while exploring the links between the two approaches (Thomas, 2007). The activities, key points and case studies are intended to provide ideas and build confidence to apply the methods in your own practice. Before introducing participation, it feels only right to provide a *health warning*. Participation could win awards for being one of the simplest of concepts, that when analysed in practice both influences and is influenced by personal, organisational and societal values.

The terms person, people or young people and children will be used to refer to those who use services. Bourdieu identified how language actively determines how people understand and value the world rather than language passively reflecting reality. The impact of language provides a useful starting point to understanding participatory practice, in particular its power to include or exclude. Each professional sector has its own language and associated jargon, which determines what is valued, what is expected and what can be questioned (Webb et al., 2002). Participatory practice requires language and information to be inclusive, accessible and broadly understandable. This introduction to participation aims to avoid academic or professional jargon and acronyms.

Understanding Participation

Defining participation

Participation has multiple meanings. It includes activities and hobbies, education and work, which then leads it towards a social or political focus linking it to citizenship and social democracy. When applied in practice to social work and social pedagogy, participation is a value-shaped dynamic process leading to action and change. The Voice Model of participation (Wyness, 2013) relies upon the quality of listening; its focus is upon people's voices being heard which then influences decision-making processes. This sounds straightforward, but complexity arises from interpretation, differing values and beliefs, professional ego and skills, and the uniqueness of individuals and individual decisions. The development of respect and trust through relationships influences the balance of power between those who provide and those who receive a service. This mutual balance is central to effective participation in decision-making. It is useful to note that participation is not about people getting everything they want. It is, however, about people being informed, expressing what they want and need, and understanding why and how that can or cannot happen.

The definitions below specifically refer to children but are equally applicable to people of all ages. The important issue to acknowledge is the difference in power between the person and those people who can influence decisions, whether they are family members or professionals.

Thomas (2007, p. 199) provides a definition of children's active participation, he states: 'Participation can refer generally to taking part in an activity, or specifically to taking part in decision-making.' It is viewed as active participation, knowing that one's actions are taken note of and may be acted upon (Boyden and Ennew, 1997). Lansdown (2011, p. 3) goes on to define this as:

An ongoing process of [children's] expression and active involvement in decision making at different levels in matters that concern them. It requires information sharing and dialogue between children and adults based on mutual respect, and requires that full consideration of their views be given, taking into account the child's age and maturity.

This analysis of participation and rights involves the principled belief that social justice is based upon respect and the equality of citizens regardless of their age (Bessell, 2001). It relies upon two beliefs: firstly that children and adults have agency. Leena Alanen (cited in Cregan and Cuthbert, 2014, p. 12) explains agency as, 'The child's ability to control and to act consciously: to be social actors or agents in their own right'. The notion of agency is applicable to both children and adults, meaning they are able to act as autonomous individuals who are motivated, skilled and able to take part in decision-making. The second belief requires practitioners to value people's involvement and have the skills to incorporate people within decision-making processes and power to act on the resulting decisions (Jones and Walker, 2011).

Thomas (2007) differentiates between *collective* and *individual* participation. Collective participation is undertaken to create change within an organisation or a community, while individual participation is focused upon the personal decisions about a person's life (for example care planning). Each of these forms of participation will be introduced and their interdependent relationship will be explored later in the chapter.

Is participation a good thing?

The benefits of participating are strongly argued. Morrow (cited in Invernissi and Williams, 2009, p. 123) states, 'Participation' is assumed to be a 'good thing' that leads to increased self-efficacy, which in turn leads to an increased awareness of choices, which contribute to improved 'well-being'. Shier (2001) cites Treseder (1997), Willow (1997) and Adams and Ingham (1998) as they identify the benefits in respect of improving the quality of services, increasing responsibility and self-esteem and engaging people as citizens, which supports democratic participation and citizenship in the longer term. An alternative view is strongly argued by Cooke and Kothari (2004, p. 1), who state participation workers talk of participatory processes undertaken ritualistically, which turn out to be manipulative, or which have in fact harmed those who are supposed to be empowered. Cooke and Kothari cite Guijt and Shah, who identified within participatory development work the concept that a community sharing common interests can mask the influence of position within a community, and the bias that can result. Cooke and Kothari (2004) go on to identify that participatory planning can in fact be constrained, shaped and manipulated by the formal and informal goals of the organisation, service or community leading the work. These opposing arguments evidence the spectrum of beliefs and opinions about participation.

The purpose of participation goes beyond benefiting the individual through the development of skills, confidence and self-esteem. Sinclair (2004) identifies how it upholds human rights; it can improve services making them more relevant; it fulfils legal duties to improve services and decision-making; it enhances democracy. Citizenship and social inclusion can be enhanced through developing the belief that people have the ability to create change and increase their awareness of rights, through political and social education (Kirby et al., 2003). This relational link between individuals and society is also a core concept of social pedagogy. In Chapter 1 we used the quote from Sunker and Braches-Chyrek (2009, cited in Stephens, 2013, p. 68) to highlight this: 'The goal of social pedagogy is, firstly, to improve the unequal social conditions by socio-political means, and secondly to enable individuals to fight their own battle to improve social conditions.'

Matthews (2003, cited in Thomas, 2007, p. 200) argues that participation is an essential and moral ingredient of any democratic society – enhancing quality of life, enabling empowerment, encouraging psychosocial well-being, and providing a sense of inclusiveness.

Concepts and Theoretical Framework

Values

The definitions above incorporate values and demonstrate how the interpretation of participation is subjectively influenced by personal values around agency and power. Smith (2005) discussed how values inform opinions about moral choice and preferred theoretical frameworks. Kirby et al. (2003) confirm values underpin practice and inform a culture of participation. Values evolve, and influence practitioners' beliefs about vulnerability and power and then shape culture and professional approaches to participation in decision-making. Everything that is shaped through values is by its very nature subjective, fluid and challenging. The concept of values is effectively captured within the philosophical framework of social pedagogy. *Haltung*, introduced in Chapter 3, is a German word that roughly translates as ethos, mindset or attitude (Eichsteller, 2010). Wieninger (2000, cited in Eichsteller, 2010) describes how a person's *Haltung* is influenced by their concept of children (or of humankind in general), by how they think about them, what notions they hold about who they are. This leads to understanding the intrinsic relationship between a practitioner's *Haltung* and their conceptualisation of people who are vulnerable or marginalised in some way. There are many references to values having an 'abstract and ethereal nature, which may account for why they are problematic to identify or discuss' (Shardwell, 1998, cited in Smith, 2005, p. 2). Values concern the 'weighty aspects in life and characterise morally desirable ways of acting in the world' (Smith, 2005, p. 29). He continues to say that values can be understood as the beliefs and principles that inform professional judgement and reflect moral choices. Dominelli (2002, cited in Smith, 2005) contributes to the discussion by stating that they have different forms ranging through cultural, professional, religious and personal aspects of society at a specific time. 'Values do not just appear as fully formed sets of principles which offer unproblematic practice guidance; they are derived from wider ideological traditions to be found within the fabric of society', argues

Smith (2005, p. 8). He also identifies the wider political and sociological influences on both individual and organisational values.

Clarke and Percy-Smith (2006, cited in Mannion, 2007, p. 405) note 'the complexity and interplay of values and interests in local decision-making and everyday social processes'. Values hold an ability to create preference, to believe one theory over another, which in turn may lead to a preferred professional approach. Smith (2005) identifies that the social construction of an activity needs to be scrutinised to understand the ideological and theoretical basis of professional values.

Childhood is a useful example to illustrate how the values held by practitioners and society influence their approach to decision-making. Developmental theory of childhood developed through the 1960s and 1970s, supported by the work of Piaget. The child is viewed as 'a passive object, raw material waiting to be molded into a later human being' (Cregan and Cuthbert, 2014, p. 11). Children's self-determination is limited by adults who 'have their needs and rights variously ascribed and constricted according to the dominant paternalistic ideologies, albeit activated for "good" and "caring" reasons' (James et al., 1998, p. 211). This value base leads to children being seen as in need of protection: they are predominantly vulnerable and children's involvement in decision-making could be constructed as inappropriate or even damaging to them. An alternative view evolved during the 1980s through the socialisation theory of childhood, which introduced the concept of *agency*, as previously explained (Alanen, 1988), and this became central to reframing children's self-determination. The concept of agency is useful for the analysis of power between adults and children and as Alanen (1988, cited in Cregan and Cuthbert, 2014, p. 13) explains, it makes us aware of 'the child's ability to control and to act consciously: to be social actors or agents in their own right'. The child is viewed as always having capabilities (Biggeri et al., 2011) and is a *being* rather than a *becoming* (James and Prout, 1990). The importance of relationships within participation is acknowledged and how 'individual children and adults must interrelate across age divisions, power inequalities and (in families) household norms and needs' (Cregan and Cuthbert, 2014, p. 12). This concept of children is expressed by the social pedagogical historical key thinker Janusk Korczak (1878–1942). His views are compatible with socialisation theory:

> Children are not the people of tomorrow, but are people of today. They are entitled to be taken seriously. They have a right to be treated by adults with respect, as equals. They should be allowed to grow into whoever they were meant to be – the unknown person inside each of them is the hope for the future. (Korczak, cited in Eichsteller, 2010, p. 7)

Shier (2001) confirms that for children to have power, adults have to concede power in favour of children. This suggests adult controls within decision-making processes are maintained in spite of the possibly genuine efforts of adults to empower children to exercise their rights. This begins to demonstrate how participation becomes complex as practitioners, organisations, families and communities hold different and sometimes conflicting values about vulnerability, agency, power and decision-making.

ACTIVITY 6.1

Our first experiences of decision making

Try to remember a decision-making experience during your childhood. For example, this could be one of the following: moving school; moving house; getting or not getting a pet; going on holiday; choosing clothes; attending an event; medical treatment; your friendships or activities.

Think about who was involved in the decision-making? Was it just one person or a shared decision?

Were you included or excluded in making this decision? Did you have agency?

Choose three words to describe the style of decision-making that you grew up with ....

How did you feel?

Your answers will indicate the value placed on your own voice as a child and the influence you had. These formative experiences of decision-making can inform the development of our personal values and beliefs about power and rights. Mannion (2007, p. 413) reports how children's participation is connected with the 'attitudes, empowerment and participation of adults ... [and that] adult participation is affected by their own childhood experiences'. Boyden (2003) argued that even under adverse circumstances children can influence the environments around them, and their experience of childhood will lead to the development of competencies. When children are viewed as being capable, as having agency and an ability to share their values, views and ideas, it is their experiences and social influences during childhood that shape their capabilities as adults. Sen (2007, cited in Biggeri et al., 2011, p. 22) adds that the 'capabilities that adults enjoy are deeply conditional on their experience as children'. It can be argued the wisdom gained in childhood leads to an early alignment with chosen values and the formation of *Haltung* reflecting their own moral choices.

KEY POINT

Participation is an approach informed through values. A participatory culture is evident when every aspect of an organisation is in tune with those values

Power

Much has been researched and written about power and many theories provide useful perspectives to make sense of the behaviour and decisions of individuals, families, communities, professionals and organisations. Bourdieu understood the power of the *everyday*, where something specific disguises itself as general and acquires status. He called this *habitus*, which is identified through becoming conscious of the unconscious. Bourdieu recognised the power asserted within everyday actions and processes that by the nature of them are routine and unquestioned. These habits through their consistency inform people's beliefs, which in turn strengthen the habit (Webb et al., 2002). This can be applied to participation in decision-making at many levels as people and their families, practitioners and managers can fall into inherited processes and predetermined positions of authority through assumption. The practitioner with a participatory ethos or *Haltung* questions systems and positions of authority and this in itself can lead to them being marginalised and viewed as trouble makers. An essential skill is communication and the effective practitioner knows their professional field of expertise, which leads them to understand what is and what is not negotiable. They hear the views of people who are marginalised and creatively enable those in positions of authority to hear those views within decision-making processes. How this partnership process is applied in practice will be explored later in this chapter.

Laverack (2009, cited in Jones and Walker, 2011, p. 143) talked of *power with*, which usefully describes effective interdependent decision-making. He talks of power being 'used carefully and deliberately to increase other people's power, rather than to dominate or exploit'. The concept of *interdependence* was introduced by Qvortrup et al. (1994). It acknowledges generational dependencies between children and adults and evidenced that children value the wisdom of adults and understand the need for guidance and at times protection. It is, however, most effectively achieved through trusting and respectful relationships with skilled competent adults (Mannion, 2007). The quality and interdependent nature of these relationships must enable the balance of power to be flexible and robust, like the qualities of an elastic band, tensing and supporting each of the individuals as the balance of power shifts in response to different times and spaces. Foucault's argument that power exists when it is exercised and active, rather than a *dormant possibility*, supports this understanding of interdependent intergenerational power (Gallagher, 2008). The powers exercised by each party through shared decision-making change, but when in balance the tension of the elastic band is relaxed and is not being felt by either party.

Linking these concepts to social pedagogical theory, the concept of Life World Orientation (Grundwald and Thiersch, 2009) was introduced in Chapter 4 in relation to risk. In considering the delicate balancing of power within a professional relationship, this concept essentially captures the importance of knowing and also understanding the perspective of the person you are working with. An effective practitioner needs to understand social problems and their impact, as they are experienced and interpreted by the people who are directly affected (Eichsteller et al., 2014). Effective interdependent decision-making requires shared respect acquired through the development of a trusting relationship. The quality of the relationship is maintained through ongoing information exchange, open questioning and honest reflection. This in turn provides a greater insight into the issues and priorities of the person you are working with. It is this insight that informs the appropriate balance of power, and in terms of the elastic band enables the level of tension to be owned and changed by both people. This tuning in is central to individual participation practice and is reflected in the value base of social pedagogy.

It is important to consider the challenges to achieving a greater balance of power. The presence of parents in decision-making can override or erode the voice of the child (Coyne et al., 2015). Staff who seek the views of children can be anxious about rejecting or challenging the views of children and may be reticent to relinquish their professional status and power (Day, 2008; Richter et al., 2009; Worrall-Davies, 2008). The dilemma of who is the person using the service and whose voice should take precedence is real for practitioners and is likely to elicit uncomfortable emotional responses that can lead to 'idiosyncratic professional practice' (Morris et al., 2009, p. 12). Conflicts of interest and incompatible agendas between stakeholders require time, skilled negotiators and sensitive but directive planning (Worrall-Davies, 2008). Even when skilled leadership is present, professionals still need to personally find their own comfortable place with participatory practice and giving up their authority (Day, 2008). The inconsistency of approaches to participatory practice reflects the variations in approaches and styles of interventions between professionals within the same team (Frith, 2016). For service transformation to be successful, attention must be paid to the interactions between individual practitioner and a child, young person or adult (Tait and Lester, 2005, cited in Richter et al., 2009).

Working in an adult mental health environment, Schwartz et al. (2013) identified a growing awareness by clinicians that people did not want to assume full control of their own care, but valued the structure and support provided by clinicians. The people using the service became aware of the challenges for the clinician who by sharing power must also readjust their understanding of their clinical responsibilities. Achieving such a balance of power is challenging for both professionals and those who use services. As a practitioner it is vital to return to the equation of what is and what is not negotiable and this must be assessed in respect of risk, legislation, professional expertise and the person's abilities and understanding.

Legal framework

The government evidences their commitment to active participation in decision-making through making it a legal duty within statute. It is a common thread running through child, adult, mental health and advocacy legislation and guidance (for example the Children Act 1989 and 2004; Human Rights Act 1998; Mental Capacity Act 2005; Mental Health Act 1983, amendments 2007; and Care Act 2014). Specific wording clarifies the legal duty of professionals to ensure 'Patients [are] fully involved in decisions about care, support and treatment' (DoH, 2015a, p. 22). The Children Act (1989), Section 17 states:

> (4A)Before determining what (if any) services to provide for a particular child in need in the exercise of functions conferred on them by this section, a local authority shall, so far as is reasonably practicable and consistent with the child's welfare – (a) ascertain the child's wishes and feelings regarding the provision of those services; and (b) give due consideration (having regard to his [sic] age and understanding) to such wishes and feelings of the child as they have been able to ascertain.

Consider how this legislation is translated into practice. There are two distinct elements to this section. The first is to find out what the child wants and feels. Using a participatory approach and working creatively can provide an individually planned method of engagement that can be decided with the child, and tailored to their interests. Secondly, the practitioner gives the wishes and feelings consideration. Remember the issues raised in respect of values, power and conflicting perspectives about children being primarily vulnerable or having agency to make decisions. In practice it is important for practitioners to reflect on their own values and cultural bias when considering or judging the wishes of a child. Creativity is again a useful method to present the views of the child to those who have influence (see this discussed in Chapter 3). Children rarely choose typed reports to express themselves, often preferring to write stories, dance, sing, draw and make films.

Although the United Nations Convention on the Rights of the Child (1989) is not legally binding, the rights of children are explicitly identified and can be seen incorporated into current child and family law. The Convention is generally viewed as a significant turning point, placing the rights of children on the political agenda globally (Jones and Walker, 2011). It does, however, have many limitations and 20 years on Lansdown (2011) confirmed the need to challenge the government to fulfil their responsibilities under the UNCRC (1989) to ensure the rights of all children to participate are consistently and actively supported. The provision of independent advocacy could be viewed as further confirmation that participation remains an aspiration. The provision of advocacy as a legal right appears in mental health and children's legislation. The significance of advocacy as a legal right acknowledges the vulnerability of some groups of people in society, and identifies listening as an appropriate response to vulnerability. It confirms a systemic power imbalance between services and those who use them.

The thread continues through service standards, such as the HCPC Social Work Standards (2017), the Social Pedagogy Professional Association Standards (SPPA, 2017), the *Independent Reviewing Officers' Handbook* (DfE, 2010) and the Care Programme Approach (2008); and also government transformation programmes like Building a Culture of Participation (2003) and the National Service Framework (2004).

Finding participation in organisations

Choose a piece of legislation, national guidance or local policy that is relevant to your work:

- An Act of Parliament that you are responsible for applying to your work, e.g. the Mental Health Act 2007, the Children Act 1989 or 2004, the Human Rights Act 1998, the Care Act 2014.
- National guidance your organisation must implement, e.g. *Working Together to Safeguard Children* (DfE, 2018b).
- An internal policy document that you are involved in delivering, e.g. safeguarding policy, assessment policy, care planning and review policy.

Is participation evident in the document?
Is it a requirement or an option?
How do you experience this in your organisation? How do you see participation in *practice* in your day-to-day work?

Theoretical Frameworks

There are many theoretical and visual representations of participation, each with their strengths and weaknesses (Creative Commons, 2012). A brief introduction to three of these follows with the intention of raising awareness rather than providing a detailed analysis. They relate to child participation through an analysis of power, which is transferrable to all people. Possibly the best known is Hart's Ladder of Participation (Hart, 1992), which he adapted from Arnstein's Ladder of Citizen Participation (1969, cited in Hart, 1992). It is easy to understand and provides a useful introduction to different hierarchical levels of participation which illustrate varying degrees of power sharing. Its weakness, as identified by Hart himself, is that participation is not a step-by-step linear process moving from *tokenism* at the bottom through to *child-initiated shared decisions* at the top (Hart, 2008). Each decision is unique by circumstance and what is appropriate participation one day may not be possible or appropriate a week later. The implication is to assume best practice and to strive at all times for the top rung. Yet this oversimplifies participation and does not take into account the differing types of participation and the needs and desires people have to participate (Jones and Walker, 2011).

Treseder (1997) developed the Degrees of Participation. This model removes the linear hierarchy of participation and acknowledges there should be no limits to participation and that children will need to be empowered to develop the skills and confidence to fully partici- pate. Hart (1992, p. 4) had also identified that for children, 'the confidence and competence to be involved must be gradually acquired through practice'. Treseder uses Hodgson's Five Conditions for Children's Participation, which are: (1) people need access to those in power; (2) access to information; (3) real choice between different options; (4) support from a trusted independent person; (5) an appeal or complaint process (Creative Commons, 2012, p. 7).

Shier (2001) developed the Pathways to Participation, which identified five levels of partici- pation each with openings, opportunities and obligations. The strength of this framework is that each stage poses a question for practitioners and managers to reflect upon. For example at stage four it asks, 'Are you ready to let children join in your decision-making processes?' It goes on to then ask if there is a procedure to enable that to happen, and further still whether there is a policy requirement that children must be involved in decision-making? The Pathways can be applied to both collective and individual participation and provides links to Hear by Right (Badham and Wade, 2005), a self-assessment tool for organisational participation.

Applying Participation

Individual participation

Decision-making is a simple concept; it is almost so obvious that it is sometimes hard to understand why it is so complex. Remember back to the first activity you did when you thought about your first experiences of decision-making as a child. *How involved were you? How was your voice heard? How much weight did your views hold?* Consider how empowered or disempowered you were and whether that came from within or was influenced by the people around you. When people use social work or social pedagogy services, it is likely they have some need that can lead to increased vulnerability that can affect their resilience. Being in this situation can reduce people's confidence and ability to voice their questions, needs and concerns effectively. This can contribute to widening the power gap between those who need to receive services and those who are there to provide them. An aim of this chapter is for practitioners to *tune in,* identify and then understand the power gap. Once this has become a professional skill it is possible to use the approaches and tools selectively to *walk alongside* the person you are working with, seeing the world from their perspective (Petrie, 2013).

Preparation for Participation

Listening

Participation with individuals begins and ends with listening and communication and is a key skill for social workers and social pedagogues (BASW, 2012; HCPC, 2017; SPPA, 2017).

Most people who drive believe they are good drivers and likewise most of us believe we are good listeners. This as you will know is not always true. Listening is also a little like playing a musical instrument, the level of skill needs to be continually maintained or we become 'rusty'.

ACTIVITY 6.3

Being heard and how it feels

Think of a time when you were really listened to.

What were the circumstances?
What did the person actually do?
How did you know you were being heard?
How did you feel?
How does this compare to when you have not been listened to?

Assumptions

Just like driving, even when it is our core job to listen old habits creep in. Making assumptions, for example, is an old habit and I frame assumption as the enemy to listening and participation as it involves making an uninformed judgement. It links closely to Bourdieu's concept of *habitus* (Webb et al., 2002). Assumptions can be made when the person may have said the same thing several times previously; you are under time pressures or about to go on annual leave. If you assume or recognise that a colleague has made an assumption, reframe it as *guessing*; and a useful antidote to assumptions or guessing is to check out your understanding with the person whose life will be affected by the decisions. Would you write a professional report and include the phrase *I didn't have time so I guessed they would no longer want to see their family*? Would you be happy for someone in your life to *guess* what you think and feel? Even more concerning is if the *guess* is then reframed as a *fact*, and that fact influences decisions in your life. Bourdieu called this the *oracle effect*, where language has impact and makes the world (Webb et al., 2002).

ACTIVITY 6.4

The dangers of assumption

Think about a time when you made an assumption and got things wrong.

Why did you get things wrong?

Did getting it wrong have an impact on you, and the person you made the assumption about?

Now think about a time when someone made an assumption about you.

How did it make you feel?
Does an assumption that turns out to be accurate, make the assumption OK?

The balance to be achieved is to listen and tune in while analysing information with professional knowledge of legislation, risk and theory. The concept of Head, Heart and Hands can support this process (Brühlmeier, 2010). The knowledge and analysis process links to the *head*. The *Haltung* of the professional creates a level of congruence, which influences the level of trust in the relationship and this links to the *heart* element. Finally, the *hands* aspect of listening is the body language and additional activities to support an open dialogue. Even with the most exceptional listening skills, participation is not about people always getting what they want and professionals being silenced; it is about combining skills and knowledge to gain the best outcome for the person from their own perspective. It is important to have considered in each professional conversation what is, and what is not negotiable. It is only through transparent communication about legal power or professionally assessed risk that people can then be supported to influence the decisions that are negotiable. There will always be situations where best interest decision-making is appropriate; as we know, there are situations where decisions have to be made without full information and without consent. Understanding this balance between safeguarding and enabling positive risk taking requires professional confidence and skill. It is important to be aware when risk is used, to override participatory practice (Lansdown, 2011). (See Chapter 7 for more discussion around this.)

 *CASE EXAMPLE 6.1*

Individual Care Planning

Sam, who is looked after by the local authority, will be moving placement in three weeks as his foster carer, Anisa, is seriously ill. The social worker, Kris, planned a conversation with Sam to focus upon his priorities for the next placement and understand his wishes and feelings (Children Act 1989). In listening to Sam his main issue was whether Anisa was going to die and whether he had contributed to her illness. Sam had already experienced loss and bereavement and could not think about his future needs, as these emotional issues were so difficult. Kris listened to

(Continued)

(Continued)

Sam's concerns and then worked with Anisa, the family placement team and Sam to share information and support him. He needed to understand the illness and prepare for the ending of the placement positively through maintaining contact with Anisa. They created a plan where Sam could help Anisa by walking her dog Muttley, while she was in hospital. With all this in place Sam could then actively participate in decisions about his own plans.

What happened here?

Kris believed Sam had agency to influence decisions in his life. This belief shaped her approach by talking directly to Sam prior to the decision-making (Table 6.1). Through this Life World Orientation approach she hoped to gain understanding of Sam's current perspective and to plan the future *with* rather than *to* the child (Grundwald and Thiersch, 2009).

The conversation was not as Kris expected, who wanted Sam's voice to influence the *matching process* for the next placement. She knew the timescales for the panel and needed to be prepared. She heard Sam's anxieties and from her knowledge of practice and theory understood Sam needed to end this placement sensitively prior to him being able to look to the future.

What happened next?

Kris obtained information about Anisa's illness and treatment, as she did not know about the condition herself. Using modelling clay, a toy medical kit and some soft toys, they sat and learnt together. Sam led the conversation and they made shapes to represent their feelings, then created stories with the toys. This helped both of them talk about Anisa and the people who had previously died. Kris *walked alongside* (Petrie, 2013) and this helped Sam believe he had not made anyone ill and Kris understood the situation better. This creative method of working led to a Common Third activity as Kris and Sam were learning together through shared creative activities. Kris was also aware of the Danish concept of the Three Ps (Jappe, 2010) as she shared her *personal* experience of bereavement but in a sensitive manner. It was in this session the plan to walk Muttley began to develop as the modelling clay was used to express fun and happiness. The impact of working together creatively led to creativity in Sam's plans. More time was taken, but the quality of the listening and the relationship reflected the quality of plan (Sinclair, 2004).

Table 6.1 Preparing to share power in decision-making

Not negotiable	Negotiable
Foster carer being ill	Gaining information and understanding
Placement will end in 3 weeks	How the next 3 weeks will support the goodbye and the move
Discussion with social worker	Where, when and how the discussion happens Deciding what are the most important things to discuss to help with decision-making
New placement	The child's essential criteria if there is a choice of placements Introductions
	What support is needed for the move to be successful

Non-participatory Approach

This simple case example above illustrates the importance of attention to what could be seen as small details. A social worker who had a less participatory approach may have reacted to the time pressure of the matching panel and arrived to talk to Sam about potential placements and the immediate impact on his school or family contact. Practitioners who are distracted by process may not consider their organisation should prioritise a reflective approach. They need to be enabled through organisational leadership, and the development of systems and structures that support reflective working (Kirby et al., 2003). If this was not in place Sam's emotional concerns regarding loss and guilt could be missed while the impending plans could increase anxiety and undermine the next placement. The differences between individual practitioners' levels of participatory approaches are complex as there are numerous variables and influences on individual practice, some more visible than others. The relational culture and value base of the organisation is a significant influence. (This is explored in more depth later in this chapter.) If Kris's managers and the processes did not value or accommodate the voice of the child there would be little if any support for this work to happen or for timescales to be stretched. Values inform the culture of the organisation, and the culture through systems and processes of decision-making creates power over both staff and the people using the services (Kirby et al., 2003). The beliefs and values of the individual worker, their *Haltung*, informs their position in respect of anti-oppressive rights-based practice. The culture of the organisation, however, can also influence individual practice. The quality of a professional's work will depend upon their skills to communicate and build purposeful relationships. How they approach the development of professional relationships will also be influenced by their personality, ego and their insight and their management of professional power. Taking all these variables into account the social worker needs to have the skills to assess and champion the views of the person they are working with. Taking this approach is courageous, as it could make them unpopular and mean greater risks will be taken. Chapter 1 introduced the philosophical ethos of the social pedagogue, where *Haltung* informs the pedagogue's approach. Power is addressed through the acknowledgement that all people have value and are equal human beings, where professional relationships are based upon inclusion and true participation. It is through creativity that organisational barriers to participation can be dismantled (Kirby et al., 2003).

Information Sharing and Safeguarding

Once a practitioner has listened and gained understanding of the issue from the person whose life is affected, it is more likely they can decide in partnership as an effective way forward. A Life World Orientation approach creates conversations where people can explore their own ability to effect change and identify what information is needed to make decisions (Jacaranda, 2015). Using a holistic approach means understanding someone else's perspective, taking into account their personality, strengths and dislikes, their view of the world, cultural influences and priorities. The development of purposeful and honest relationships can lead to a balancing and flexing of power where true partnership working can blossom. Balancing children's rights with their need for protection is complex and challenging (Lansdown, 2011). It is most effectively achieved through trusting and respectful relationships with skilled, competent adults (Mannion, 2007). Through the development of mutually respectful relationships, communication and information sharing is able to flow effectively in both directions. Once people have been listened to and their views respected, they have an experience of trust and are in a position to assess whether to share information in the future (Participation Works, 2007). This trusting, respectful process contained within relationships can reduce risk, through increasing people's confidence in their own voice. Taking a participatory approach links directly to safeguarding vulnerable children and adults (DfE, 2018b). Participation through communication then moves from the individual conversation into the systems and processes of organisations. There is a risk of the person's voice becoming lost and less influential in decisions about their lives. Managers, colleagues, partner professionals and legal teams may all have different views about what is and what is not negotiable. Information flow and language may be biased in one direction; meeting times and agendas can favour professionals at the expense of the person whose life is affected. Building a culture of participation throughout an organisation can address these issues and prevent the marginalisation of people's voices. Creating such a culture 'is a complex and dynamic process. Change has to be negotiated between policy makers, senior managers, other staff and [younger] people. This is a creative process that involves eliciting and fostering enthusiasm, sharing ideas and learning through doing' (Kirby et al., 2003, p. 24).

 *CASE EXAMPLE 6.2* ▬▬▬▬▬▬▬▬▬▬▬▬▬▬▬▬

Individual Decision-making in Formal Processes

This framework and process has been co-designed in partnership with young people, families and staff. Acknowledgement is made that it relates to a formal process of decision-making. The practice relates to multi-agency office-based meetings; however the principles are transferrable to formal decision-making meetings held in family homes and other informal environments. The framework has developed through decades of experience of attending and chairing formal decision-making meetings. There are several stages of informal decision-making prior to, and running parallel with, the main care planning decision-making process. Formal decision-making processes tend to use the method of meetings and are defined through legislation such as the Children Act 1989 and 2004, leading to the Independent Reviewing Service for Looked After Children (DfE, 2010). Within mental health services the formal process is known as the Care Programme Approach (CPA).

There are three distinct stages in the framework and it is useful to think of them as a cycle that continues throughout the care planning process. These are identified as:

- Preparation pre decision-making
- Decision-making to develop the plan
- Post decision-making action, change and review.

Stage 1: Preparation

Aims:

Prepare with the person for their meeting.
Review the current plan to inform the agenda and attendance at the decision-making stage.
Review and distribute information needed to inform decision-making.
Design the meeting environment and structure and style of the meeting.

Method:

1   Identifying the chair or facilitator of the meeting is essential. Clarity is needed to understand whether they are independent or have a stake in the decision-making

(Continued)

(Continued)

as the power held by the chair needs to be transparent. In practice, the date, time and venue may have been predetermined. Ideally this will have been influenced by the person to ensure they feel comfortable and confident and it is not scheduled to conflict with something important to them.

2   Reviewing the care plan. The simplest way to begin this process is to ensure that an accurate and current care plan is available and to meet with the person to check progress and consider priorities for the future. This stage of preparation can be useful to identify the person's level of confidence, and consider their role from co-chairing the meeting through to needing an independent advocate.

3   Agenda. The above discussion should identify the person's priorities, which should inform the agenda. Further discussion with family, friends and colleagues will also contribute to the agenda. Once this is complete, the person, working with the chair, should place the items in their preferred order of preference and allocate time to each item. This indicates how important or complex the person perceives each item to be. Communication between the chair and the person whose meeting it is significantly contributes to the person's voice being central to the decision-making. It is useful to discuss the most important priority and also any subjects the person does not wish to discuss or decide in a meeting. This discussion can identify creative methods for the person to share their views at the meeting. To share their views and priorities in meetings children and adults have used creative methods including film, newsletters, poetry, painting and drawing and animation; the possibilities are endless.

A clear link to social pedagogy and creativity can be made here. As discussed in previous chapters, to support people with their well-being, learning and growth we need to build positive and supportive relationships and creativity is a big part of this. Jan Storø (2013) writes that creativity and creative activities are an important place where social pedagogues can support people to learn new skills and knowledge that they can apply to other parts of their lives. To approach formal decision-making meetings as an opportunity for creativity has many benefits. It can reduce both the boredom and anxiety experienced by many people when preparing to make decisions in this process-driven way. It creates choice and activity between the worker and the person, which can support the development of trust and information sharing. These positive outcomes culminate in increased engagement in the process. It creates rehearsal time where thoughts can be processed and most importantly it is fun.

4   Attendance. The person has identified their priorities and the rest of the agenda and it is now the attendance can be determined to support the decision-making. The priority on the agenda should indicate the most important people needing to attend and it is useful to keep the numbers low as this provides a

more comfortable environment for the person and family and professionals to communicate. It is at this stage negotiation may need to take place to change the date, time or venue to ensure essential people can attend or send information if they are unable to.

There may be someone who wants or needs to attend but who the person chooses not to meet with. Children may not want their divorced parents in the room. Young people over 16 years of age using health services can exclude their parents, which can be challenging when the parents need to understand and manage risk. These situations require creativity and negotiation, as split meetings are possible. Availability of the independent advocate needs to be checked and arrangements made if required.

There should be no surprises and the person should know who is attending and ideally have met each person. They need to understand the roles, responsibilities and authority of each person in relation to the current and future care plan. Where invitation letters or emails are sent it is useful to notify services that only the person invited is expected to attend. Practitioners can arrive with their manager or a student without previously checking but assuming this is acceptable. Asking the person at the point of entering the meeting places unhelpful pressure and potential anxiety on them, and if several people do this, a meeting planned with six people can quickly become 10 people. The skill of the chair is important as professionals and family members may need to be turned away before entering the room.

5   Information sharing. Ideally all those attending should have a copy of the care plan and the agenda and also any supporting reports or documents which they read in advance of the meeting. This reduces the time of the meeting and enables people to formulate questions and answers prior to the meeting.

6   Designing the meeting – things to consider:

Venues are important as places can inhibit or provide a safe, comfortable environment. Schools for example can be a safe haven for a child and enable teachers to attend. They can also be intimidating for parents and professionals and confidentiality can be at risk. When a person is detained on an acute ward the venue may be limited but the person may have choice over which room is used and how the furniture is arranged. Tables are important to consider as a conference-style table can impede open discussion. They provide a physical barrier between people and can demonstrate hierarchy as professionals spread their files, diaries and now laptops in front of them.

Seating arrangement. This is possibly one of the simplest and most effective methods to maximise a person's feeling of comfort and control of an

(Continued)

(Continued)

environment. The person designs the seating and decides where people will sit. This enables them to place themselves in the most comfortable location in the room and decide who sits next to them and across where they will have the most eye contact. Name cards can be used or a seating plan made available for everyone to follow. In practice this works very well and symbolically represents the person has opinions and authority to make decisions in the process.

Refreshments. The person whose meeting it is can decide about refreshments and may choose to prepare them. Their importance will be influenced by the wishes of the person and also the time of the meeting and the distances people have travelled.

Breaks and split meetings. The care plan, agenda and attendance will provide an indication of the length of time needed for the meeting and whether the process needs to be designed in several stages, with people attending part or all of the meeting. An example of this is where a young person will not be in the same room as a parent. The meeting is designed to enable the child to be in for the majority of the meeting and then leaves before the parent joins the meeting. The parent then leaves for the child to return for the summary. This requires planning and a competent chair or facilitator.

Style of chairing. The chair and the person meet to discuss the preferred style of the meeting. This is where partnership working is essential and the chair needs to understand the needs and potential triggers of the person whose life is being discussed. A formal style may be needed where people attending are likely to create tension or conflict. The chair needs to know how the person will communicate if they need a break or for a discussion to be stopped. Another style is for the chair to shadow the person and support them to chair their own meeting. This requires additional preparation, but the process leads to significant advantages for the person, who ultimately facilitates their own decision-making. The discussions are directed *to* the person not *about* the person, which leads to an effective, respectful decision-making process. This style has been particularly successful where the person has been in conflict with services. They have been empowered to ask their own questions of professionals, which has led to more open discussion and can then reduce conflict.

Stage 2: The decision-making meeting

Aims:

Create a comfortable environment, which supports open and respectful discussion and decision-making.

Review the care plan and identify recommendations and agree decisions.

Identify tasks and timescales to enable progress.

Method:

1   The environment for the meeting. It is useful for the person to have visited the room in advance and make decisions about the layout of the furniture. It is also useful to check the temperature is comfortable and possibly open or close windows or turn heating up or down. If there is a seating plan and refreshments, these can be prepared. Consider reducing distractions such as external noise or activities.

     In addition to the room it is useful to identify an area where those attending can wait, and where copies of the seating plan, agenda, reports and the care plan are available on request.

2   Entering the room first should be the person with a chosen supportive person if they wish. The chair or a worker can then invite the people waiting to join the meeting and remind them of the seating plan.

3   The chair begins with the introductions, apologies and the plan of the meeting, including any breaks or refreshments and the time the meeting will end. It is also useful to share the priority of the meeting and any subjects the person has stated they do not wish to be discussed.

4   The chair then works through each item as planned with the person whose care plan is being reviewed, in the style they have agreed.

5   To summarise: each decision to progress the care plan is clarified by identifying the person or service who will take responsibility, with an agreed timescale.

6   The distribution of the information from the meeting is then negotiated. It cannot be assumed the person is comfortable with all the content of the meeting being shared with all parties. They need to be aware of who will have access to their personal information, and may decide to share all or part with some agencies or family members. Paper copies of the care plan and reports may also be recalled.

Stage 3: Post decision-making action and change

Aims:

Update the care plan.

Support the action and change process as identified through the decision-making.

(Continued)

(Continued)

Method:

1   Information from the meeting should be shared efficiently and in accessible language. The draft meeting notes prepared by the chair are checked by the person whose meeting it was and amendments are negotiated before the document is distributed.
2   The tasks identified are progressed with each participant continuing to inform and involve the person as agreed.
3   The progress made is summarised and shared in advance of the next decision-making meeting to assist with next pre-meeting review of the care plan.

Organisational Participation

This is shaped by the values and culture of an organisation. This may be an obvious statement; however in practice the culture or ethos of an organisation can be both complex and challenging to identify. 'Values do not just appear as fully formed sets of principles, which offer unproblematic practice guidance; they are derived from wider ideological traditions to be found within the fabric of society' (Smith, 2005, p. 8). Values can be a challenge to identify. Many services demonstrate their values through a mission statement or *value badge* to the people they serve, identifying their commitment to a quality of service delivery. Smith (2005, p. 1) also identified how the application of values in everyday practice is challenging. He describes them as 'nebulous and confusing'. We tend to understand the culture of an organisation through a variety of different experiences, ranging from concrete and practical to highly subjective. For an organisation to function with an ethos of participation, it must maintain a dynamic that positively seeks change and embraces opportunities to learn and improve through reflective evaluation. The relationship between values, communication and action within organisational participation is defined as follows:

> A culture of participation describes how participation sits within an organization. It reflects the values that underpin participatory practice and the reasons for involving [young] people, when and how participation is used, and the extent to which [young] people are listened to and appropriate action is taken. (Kirby et al., 2003, p. 15)

This definition provides useful pointers to identify where an organisation might sit in respect of its participatory ethos, culture or approach. Using Pestalozzi's theory of Head, Heart and Hands (Brühlmeier, 2010), this definition helps illustrate how participation and social pedagogy organically combine. Firstly the authors use the word within: this can be interpreted as the *heart* of the organisation, a vital organ that functions almost without consciousness and while reflecting the values it also represents the emotional intelligence of the organisation.

Understanding the reasons why the participation of people is important to an organisation represents the *head* element of the theory. The reasons why are often a combination of internal and external influences such as legislation, statutory guidance, research, social, political and economic circumstances, professional standards, etc. When an organisation is open to learning and change, its values and beliefs become navigation tools through the competing and conflicted influences towards an intellectually informed vision. Finally the definition includes the practical aspects of when and how people are enabled to participate, the *hand* of participation. All three aspects are essential and need to complement and support each other to maintain that vital organisational dynamic of participation, learning and change.

Understanding organisational participation is important to everyone who uses a service directly, is employed by an organisation, or lives in a community. Taking social work as an example, it is governed politically, socially and economically through legislation, national standards, guidance and policy with identifiable processes linking national to local government. Numerous pieces of legislation and guidance establish a duty or a responsibility on local services to deliver services in partnership using a participatory approach (Children Act 1989 and subsequent Children Acts; *Working Together to Safeguard Children*, 2018; Mental Health Act 2007; Care Act 2014).

Assessment frameworks to identify and measure organisational participation have developed such as: *You're Welcome* (DoH, 2017) and Investing in Children (2013). Some years ago Hear by Right provided standards and a comprehensive framework for self-assessing the 'active involvement of children and [young] people' (Badham and Wade, 2005, p. 2). It remains relevant today, beginning with an examination of organisational values. The purpose and different reasons for participation are varied:

- Adherence to legislation, convention and guidance.
- Services will be relevant and more effective which saves money.
- Empowerment and supporting the development of self-efficacy.
- Enabling the development of skills (practical and confidence).
- Contributing to the development of democratic communities (Kirby et al., 2003).

It is also useful to consider what organisations do to achieve a culture of participation:

- Management/leadership style is accessible, listening, learning and non-hierarchical. Participation includes staff, managers, people who use services and their families.
- Risk is positively managed with clear accountability, support and evaluation.
- Decision-making is transparent and accessible.
- Information sharing processes and communication are transparent, jargon free and flowing in all directions.
- Information and policies are co-written and implemented with all stakeholders.
- Recruitment processes involve stakeholders at all levels (where services are provided then those people who receive the service actively contribute to the development of job roles through to recruitment).

- The organisation is always learning through evaluation and specific training. All stakeholders are involved in the evaluation design and analysis, the development and delivery of training.

The following six categories are used within the Hear by Right tool (Badham and Wade, 2005): Strategies, Structures, Systems, Staff, Skills and Knowledge and finally Style of Leadership. It is vital to consider the style of leadership. Leaders hold power and responsibility and where leadership is open and eager to learn in partnership with the people who use the service it is likely to influence the shape of the service. The power held through leadership can effectively develop a strategy for participation that explicitly identifies the resources and strategic plan to ensure participation is embedded.

The strategy provides a visible commitment alongside the value or mission statement to evidence in more detail how the values of the organisation will translate into day-to-day practice. It needs to be developed, implemented and evaluated in partnership with all stakeholders to ensure shared ownership.

Structures and systems must be in place to support the aspirations of the strategy. The structures identify where, what and how people will participate in shared decision-making. The decision-making structures are of little use without the systems to ensure people receive and share information to make decisions. An information sharing process document is important to ensure the flow of information is in all directions, and to move away from top-down only communication.

The final two areas to assess are 'Skills and Knowledge' by considering staff recruitment and training. For a culture of participation to flourish organisations can use their recruitment processes to attract people who hold participation values and aspirations. This is achieved through job descriptions and person specifications, and recruitment processes from short-listing through to appointment.

Finally an organisation will have a prioritised training programme that includes specific participatory training designed and delivered by people who use the service. Professionals need to know and understand the decision-making structures that both support and restrict decision-making within an organisation. This ensures people are only engaged in decision-making processes in which they are in fact included. To falsely raise people's expectations about the influence they can have in decision-making will negatively impact on trust and damage the current and future professional relationships.

KEY POINT

Collective participation and individual participation are relational: there is a flow of value-based influence between organisations and communities and the individuals within them. *Haltung* is useful to conceptualise this influence. An organisation based upon the values of social pedagogy will reflect this in its approach to power in, for example, decision-making; this in turn will influence the experience of both employees and the people who use the services. The *Haltung* between the organisation and the individual will mirror each other and grow stronger.

Alternatively there can be difference between the *Haltung* of an organisation and the *Haltung* of individuals. Some organisations create oppressive regimes, which conflict with and compromise the values of individuals connected with them. In these circumstances practitioners will experience this friction and may decide to distance themselves or decide to influence and change from within. When the people who use the service experience this friction, the options are likely to be limited.

The Importance of Evaluation and Learning

Evaluation of each aspect of participatory work is essential to inform the cyclical process of learning and change. Once the aims of the work are identified it is important to design the evaluation plan. An integrated evaluation provides information during the life of the project and enables dynamic flexibility through evidenced-based reflection as the work progresses (Lansdown and O'Kane, 2014). The process of organisational change is informed through evaluation and is helpfully understood through Senninger's Learning Zone model (Jacaranda, 2015); organisations can become trapped within their comfort zone of everyday routines that manage priorities. To introduce change or uncertainty requires an organisation to move into the learning zone where it may experience challenge. As mentioned, Bourdieu's fundamental concept of *habitus* is useful in understanding the power of routines and historical ways of doing things that become invisible as second nature. This provides an introduction to the complexity of unpicking and understanding the theory of resistant power (Thomas, 2007). It is vital to have confident and bold leadership who through evaluation can provide evidence to steer an organisation through these stages of change while avoiding the panic zone where learning becomes frozen. For change to happen, the leadership will require courageous and creative staff and managers to be onboard (Kirby et al., 2003).

Outcomes evaluation

The evaluation of the outcome of the work will be determined by the focus of the work and its initial aims. What needs to be measured to identify a positive outcome? How will change and improvement be assessed? Working out these key questions is essential to the work being relevant and also having impact. If, for example, the work is to improve information about a service it will be useful to understand what people want to know. As the work progresses new aims may evolve and the evaluation needs to be responsive to these developments. The process to review the aims, progress and evaluation needs to be built into the plan. It is important to consider who will be the audience receiving this evaluation. This should inform the focus, as well as methods used to collate and present the information.

Participatory process evaluation

This part of the evaluation is focused on the participatory process of the project rather than the outcomes. How will the quality of participation be evaluated? How inclusive is each stage of the work? The participation strategy will contain organisational standards and it is against these that the quality of the work needs to be measured (Lansdown, 2004). This evaluation informs participatory practice for the future. An example of a participation evaluation could be to reflect on the methods used to engage the stakeholders. Did questionnaires, interviews or a meeting work most effectively? What could have improved the process? Most importantly, the impact of participation must be evaluated with the indicators being determined by the people who use the service (Lansdown, cited in Percy-Smith and Thomas, 2010).

Conclusion

To conclude, this chapter has explored an introduction to participation as it relates to social work and social pedagogy with a focus on the Voice Model of participation in decision-making. It is hoped this will lead to further study as availability of many theoretical frameworks with their strengths and weaknesses have been signposted. Acknowledgement of the political nature of participation has been made and that participation in practice begins and ends with individuals through their values and approaches to people and power. It is complex and constantly changing due to the nature of human values and has a reflexive relationship with organisational and community culture. The quality of organisational leadership and the relationship between individual and organisational *Haltung* have a significant impact on the development and sustainability of a culture of participation. Having a participatory ethos and approach is central to both a social worker and a social pedagogue.

Participation weaves through social work legislation and practice and professional standards. The key thinkers who have contributed to social pedagogy write about people being equal, about professional hierarchy being managed to address power differences, and about social justice (see Chapter 2). Many of the established social pedagogy theories use a participatory approach and can be used to help people develop skills and confidence in participatory methods of working (e.g. creativity, Learning Zone, Life World Orientation). Finally, participation is creative, dynamic, exciting and fun. Its messy unpredictability leads to amazing and sometimes unimaginable outcomes for people. People's experience of finding their voice can be literally life changing.

SOCIAL PEDAGOGY AND RISK
'HAVE YOU DONE A RISK ASSESSMENT?'

ALI GARDNER

This question, often posed with an ironic tone, will be very familiar for those working in social care, reflecting the pervasiveness of a risk discourse that dominates practice in the name of protecting vulnerable children and adults. Smith (2005, p. 4) suggests that this is 'symptomatic of this collective, essentially fearful state of mind'. This high degree of risk consciousness (Kemshall, 2002) has undoubtedly impacted on the role of those charged with responsibilities to protect and safeguard. Cree and Wallace (2005) suggest that this intrusion of a risk averse culture leads to social workers being afraid to show creativity and initiative as they become overly concerned with self-protection. As a result, risk is often conceptualised as a separate entity, requiring standardised professional assessments and risk management tools to identify and minimise or remove that risk. Within the field of criminal justice both with adults and children, the use of predictive risk indicators has been employed for several years with little success and has lead to increasing the numbers of individuals being brought into the criminal justice system (Goldson and Muncie, 2015). There are now efforts towards using predictive risk tools in social work with children and their families aimed at early identification of harmful situations or behaviour (Keddell, 2018). For those in receipt of protection, the experience is largely governed by procedurally driven, somewhat inflexible processes that seek to standardise or regulate practice and minimise risk, allowing limited space for the individual to influence or decide on the course of action. Returning to the question, *have you done a risk assessment?* surely epitomises the paternalistic approach to working with risk whereby the expertise is firmly located with the professional. The role is essentially understood to be something professionals *do* to the individual. Making decisions about risk is further complicated by the fact that the person or group making the decision is not always the person or group affected by the risk (Neill et al., 2008). At this point, it is important to acknowledge the power present in many decisions relating to risk that may present a threat to certain freedoms or choices for individuals. In traditional risk assessments, the power is firmly located with the professional, and the individual is often perceived as the passive recipient in this exchange. This initial positioning of power, or lack of it, is likely to determine every future aspect of the intervention and as a result reduces the likelihood of the individual taking ownership and directing decisions and actions.

Legislation, Policy and Risk

In more recent years, we have seen an emergence of legislative and policy narrative promoting service user voice, choice and self-determination. In both children and adult social work, there is a clearer emphasis on involving individuals at every stage of their social care journey, including circumstances where risk has been identified.

Safeguarding children and the law

Within the field of social care relating to the work undertaken with children and their families, there are several key pieces of legislation and policy that identify the need to assess and manage risk within the remit of safeguarding children. The cornerstone and most influential is the Children Act (1989), which contains the legal obligations around the safeguarding and protection of all children. This key piece of legislation sets out the legal duties and, as outlined by Laird (2010), also means the creation of a set of principles that underpin the work of social workers. Clearly the Children Act (1989) places a legal duty on professionals to safeguard and manage risk but also affords social workers unprecedented levels of power to intervene in the lives of vulnerable children and their families. The ideology behind this is that subsequent governments have promoted the idea that all risks are identifiable and manageable and is backed up by the obsession with evidence-based practice promoted by the New Labour government (Featherstone et al., 2014). The Children Act (2004) and policies such as *Working Together to Safeguard Children* (DfE, 2018b) give clear guidance on the role of professionals in relation to their work around risk minimisation and protection of children set against evidence-based practice. The guiding principles contained within the Children Act (1989) include partnership and joint decision-making with families, striving for non-intervention and the avoidance of court proceedings, underpinned by the *no order principle* and that the welfare of the child is of paramount consideration. These principles have played a key part in the development of social care practice with regard to identifying and managing risk, but it is the legal threshold of *significant harm* contained within the Act that has had the greatest impact on how social workers manage risk. The Children Act (1989) introduced the concept of *significant harm* and that in the best interests of the child's welfare, social workers must investigate the likelihood that a child(ren) has or is likely to suffer significant harm. Despite the introduction of this legal duty, there remained an expectation for social workers to incorporate the principles discussed above in any intervention. Evidence of a sharp rise in the numbers of children and their families subjected to assessments that have become investigative rather than supportive in nature might suggest that this has not always been the case (Bilson et al., 2017). Arguably, the lack of specific legal definitions of the terms risk and significant harm has challenged social work practitioners working against a backdrop of risk averse policies and conditions, discussed earlier in the chapter. The exposure of high profile cases where there has been the death or serious injury of a young child along with the highly charged media attention in this area has undoubtedly contributed to the profession's response to this issue.

No one would argue against the need to help protect vulnerable children and promote their well-being and development, yet the subject of risk assessment and safeguarding has become an emotive topic. There continues to be changes with regard to key legislation, with the most current being the new Children and Social Work Act (2017), which sets out a number of significant changes to the safeguarding practices and the requirements on professionals. This new Act has removed the Local Safeguarding Boards and replaced them with Child Safeguarding Practice Review Panels and places the management of safeguarding practices onto the local authority, the Clinical Commissioning Group (Health) and the Chief Officer of Police with the idea that these are the most significant public service partners best placed to respond to safeguarding needs in their local areas and provide adequate response and share information (Hayes, 2017). However, there are concerns that these new changes may well disregard the important partnership working that already exists in local areas between key agencies. Whilst it is likely that the partners identified above will play a key role in safeguarding children in their area, the focus appears to be on managing safeguarding as a process rather than recognising the individual nature and experience from the perspective of the individual and family.

Safeguarding adults and the law

From an adult's perspective, the introduction of the Mental Capacity Act in 2005 called for the inclusion of individuals in any decision relating to their life whether or not they had the capacity to do so or not. It was an important shift as the starting point was to assume capacity and to guard against blanket decisions being taken in regard to people perceived to be lacking capacity. Although the Act has led to a more inclusive, co-productive approach to decision-making, it is true to say that the notion of risk and capacity has continued to challenge professionals working with competing priorities of promoting choice and protecting vulnerable adults. The Care Act (2014) introduced a duty to promote well-being. This principle defined in Section 1 of the Act identified nine domains of well-being which included *protection from abuse and neglect* and *control by the individual of their day-to-day life*. At the same time, the Act introduced a specific safeguarding duty under Section 42, requiring the local authority to *make whatever enquiries necessary* where there is reasonable cause to suspect abuse and the individual is unable to protect themselves. This has challenged social workers faced with the question of risk, as they balance, potentially opposing, requirements both within the Care Act (2014) and additionally with the application of the Mental Capacity Act (2005) and the Human Rights Act (1998). An area where this has commonly presented itself is around self-neglect, which is included within the definition of abuse in relation to Section 42 but is frequently contested in relation to establishing capacity under the Mental Capacity Act (2005).

Challenging Conceptualisations of Risk

Whilst there are clear distinctions in how social workers respond to risk with children and adults, in relation to the level of responsibility regarding intervention, it is fair to say that the conceptualisations of risk are based largely on the professional's perspective and also greatly influenced by 'excessive rules and procedures, or the revision of performance targets' (Featherstone et al., 2012a, p. 618). Eichsteller and Holthoff (2009) assert that risk needs to start from the individual's perspective rather than the social worker's. The use of the social pedagogical concept Life World Orientation (Grundwald and Thiersch, 2009), which is rooted in critical hermeneutics, requires the social worker to understand the lived reality of the person they are completing the risk assessment with. Life World Orientation sets out the importance of understanding social problems and the impact of these on the lives of the people they are working with. The key focus of this concept is the recognition that there is no shared lived reality, instead the practitioner must use their skills to question and explore the reality for the individual. Understanding how the individual experiences and views the world around them enables the social worker to gain a better insight into how an individual is coping with everyday life situations as well as the more challenging ones. Schugurensky (2014) suggests that adapting the four dimensions set out in the Life World Orientation – time, space, social relations and cultural interpretations – can inform the assessment of risk and the responses to it. In this way, the individualised assessment would determine the social pedagogic action appropriate to the given situation. This does not mean discarding risk altogether, but rather distinguishing between risks that enhance development and well-being and those that do not. Clearly, there is still a danger of professional subjectivity and a tendency to reduce harm rather than focus on potential opportunities (Kemshall, 2002). In their work with young people, Eichsteller and Holthoff (2009, p. 10) suggested that for a child's holistic development and well-being, 'the consequences of not taking risks are more severe than the potential dangers in risk taking'

If we acknowledge that the primary aim of social work practice is to promote well-being, located within a rights-based perspective, then the role of the professional shifts to one of supporting the individual to learn about potential dangers and to develop strategies to manage those dangers rather than be absolutely protected from them in advance. Within this framework the emphasis of the practitioner's responsibility is one of development and not just of protection. Smith (2014) states that social pedagogy views risk taking as an educational objective and stresses the importance of critical reflection as a way of understanding events and interactions. In their work with children, Eichsteller and Holthoff (2009) refer to the term *risk competence* to describe the process whereby children become more knowledgeable and skilled in assessing risks and therefore acquire the competence to take risks more safely. This starts from a rights-based perspective supported by Malaguzzi's (1993) notion of the *rich child*, the belief that children possess a richness of abilities, knowledge and skills and the potential to become *risk competent* if given the opportunity. It is with this in mind that we return to the Learning Zone model presented by Senninger (2000, in Eichsteller and Holthoff, 2017) discussed in Chapter 3. The Learning Zone model begins with the comfort zone in which risk is absent and surroundings, activities and relationships are familiar and comfortable. As risk presents a degree of anxiety, it is important that we establish what the comfort zone looks like and feels like for the individual. This may become necessary if the individual needs to return or retreat to this zone during the learning process. The role of the practitioner, however, is to support the individual to move into the learning zone and then gradually to the edges of the learning zone where they will have the opportunity to experience situations or activities which they may not have conquered or achieved in the past. As the individual experiences new situations, the practitioner may encourage the person forward or to *catch* them as they *fall* back to avoid them slipping into the panic zone. The learning is very specific to the individual and does not require or benefit from the practitioner as a leader or expert but rather as an enabler or navigator. This subtle but significant shift is central to the success of the individual taking risks and learning from doing so, hence, acquiring *risk competence*. The achievement of the activity or the sense of survival of taking a risk not only provides evidence to the individual of their competence but also provides knowledge, skills and self-confidence to promote future personal development. Clearly this is not something that can take place quickly and the emphasis has to be on working at the individual's pace, something that is rarely afforded in social work, particularly at the point of assessment. We will return to the issue of clashing agendas and competing priorities impacting on risk later in the chapter.

Working Positively Alongside Risk

In order to examine the positive use of the Learning Zone model when working alongside risk, we will first explore the Making Safeguarding Personal agenda in relation to adults and then consider *Working Together to Safeguard Children* (DfE, 2018b) in relation to children.

Making Safeguarding Personal (MSP) was a sector-led initiative that has now been embedded into the Care Act (2014) and is articulated within the Safeguarding chapter within the

Statutory Guidance (DoH, 2018). MSP asserts that a cultural shift is required to deliver person-centred, outcome-based practice in relation to safeguarding. Essentially the shift is towards conversations leading processes rather than processes (paperwork and systems) leading the conversation. It recognises that individuals are experts in their own lives and the role of professionals is to work alongside individuals in responding to safeguarding situations, in a way that enhances an individual's involvement, choice and control whilst improving the quality of their life, well-being and safety.

Using the Learning Zone model in relation to this shift, both the individual and the practitioner are learning together. The comfort zone for the practitioner may be to follow protocol within existing paperwork, triggering the right questions to complete the risk assessment. In the comfort zone, the practitioner is confident that the questions will cover all aspects and reveal the information required to reduce the risk and make the person safer. Moving into the learning zone, however, the professional may well experience a level of discomfort as they enable the individual to lead the process. This will require listening and learning from the person and using their curiosity to understand their perspective. It will mean letting go of previous conceptualisations and standard responses as they work creatively towards responding to the wishes of the individuals whilst balancing this with their understanding of risk and safety. This is no easy task as further considerations such as mental capacity and risk to others will also need to be explored whilst maintaining a person-centred approach.

From the individual's perspective, an understanding of all three zones is important. Firstly, there may well be a need to return to the comfort zone as a *safe haven*. The professional can support the person to feel immediately safe and to provide reassurance. The next step, for the professional, may be to support the individual to move towards the learning zone so that they can explore their own wishes and outcomes of the safeguarding process for the long term. This may be troubling for the individual as it could mean that some risks remain or that difficult conversations are needed, perhaps challenging existing relationships with those who are perpetrators in the situations. The role of the professional is to support the individual in managing the levels of insecurity presented and ensuring that as much control remains with them at all times. It is essential, therefore, that the professional always sees themselves as a learner to avoid the danger of seeing oneself solely as the expert. Managing the shift from leading, managing and coordinating cases to enabling, facilitating, negotiating and connecting can be both liberating and challenging.

With regard to the new Children and Social Work Act (2017) and the *Working Together to Safeguard Children* (WTSC) (DfE, 2018b) policy document, the key concept of the child's best interest and supporting them to be safe is again a central theme.

The Learning Zone model supports the social worker in meeting these legal obligations whilst incorporating a child-centred approach into safeguarding, as point 13 of the introduction to WTSC (DfE, 2018b, p. 10) clearly states – children want to be *heard and understood*. This ties in with the key principles of social workers having due regard for the wishes of a child, set out in Section 22(4) of the Children Act (1989) and the United Nations Convention on the Rights of the Child (1989), which states that children have the right to expression and to receive information. In order to undertake effective assessments as required under the WTSC (DfE, 2018b) policy, the social worker must therefore balance their own professional insights and accountability alongside the views and wishes of the individual child and family. This can present challenges for both the social worker and the child and their family especially where there is a difference of perspective or understanding of a perceived risk. The Learning Zone model provides a framework for both the practitioner and the individual to explore these interpretations and to formulate actions in relation to safeguarding.

From the practitioner's perspective, it is important to become self-aware of each zone and recognise the factors that lead to a sense of panic, such as the risk averse contexts that many social workers find themselves working within. Cree and Wallace (2005) suggest this prevents practitioners from adopting creativity within their work and using their initiative. As a response there is a danger that the social worker returns to the comfort zone, where there is a greater focus on procedure, accountability and self-protection. At this point the opportunity to learn with the individual by listening and experimenting becomes unlikely and risk management rather than risk competence becomes the key focus of the intervention. From the individual's perspective, risks may be perceived in very different ways and it is important that both the individual and the practitioner enter the learning zone together to explore these perspectives. Likewise, it is important for the practitioner to understand what the comfort zone looks like for an individual. It is possible that some professionally perceived risks may represent comfort for a child. Even those relationships that might be harmful or destructive may still be perceived as familiar and comfortable to the child. It is important that the practitioner acknowledges the lived experience of the child as described in the Life World Orientation model, discussed above. It is very likely that panic for a child may be the threat of being removed or losing a parent who is viewed as problematic or unsuitable by professionals. Likewise, a parent may be placed in the panic zone at the thought of attending a formal meeting or facing an action plan for parenting. Featherstone et al. (2012b) report on parents being set measurable targets aimed at demonstrating changes in behaviour and parenting capacity which lack flexible, practical and emotional support. It is therefore essential that the practitioner understands the subtlety and complexity of comfort and panic along with recognising that, at times, the two may coexist.

The Learning Zone model encourages the practitioner to support the individual to reach the learning zone where there are opportunities to explore and experiment. It is clear, therefore, that learning has to be a joint process in which the child is listened to and encouraged to take opportunities, develop skills and understanding to keep themselves safe, or the parent is supported to identify their own, rather than imposed, solutions. The practitioner is learning about the child's lived world in order to support them in developing strategies that aim to promote their well-being whilst keeping them safe. The process of learning enables a person/family-centred rather than systems-centred approach to safeguarding. One of the key challenges to this approach is the role of power. For learning to happen, power and expertise have to be shared between the practitioner and the individual. Children need to feel a sense of control in their own lives whilst feeling supported by the adults around them. Parents need to feel ownership and confidence in their parenting roles. This is extremely difficult in cases where there are serious concerns about risks and harm. Despite any intervention, even in cases where individuals may feel decisions are made against their will, the opportunity to be listened to and to develop risk competence and positive strategies is key to working positively and respectfully with young people and their families.

Adopting a Social Pedagogical Approach to Working with Risk

In order to adopt the role as enabler and navigator and to create a conducive environment for learning in relation to risk taking, the practitioner needs to reflect on their personal perceptions of risk in order to engage with the professional task. The Three Ps model (Jappe, 2010), discussed in Chapter 3, can be used to support practitioners in reflecting on and addressing any influence they may be inadvertently exerting in their work with individuals. Eichsteller and Holthoff (2009) suggest that addressing the personal strand of the Three Ps is an important stage in supporting individuals to develop risk competence. They encourage practitioners to ask key questions such as *what do I perceive as risk?, what are my realities to this*? and *what are my boundaries to risk?* As we established in Chapter 3, the use of self and utilising a relationship-based approach to one's work is central to social pedagogical practice. Feilberg (2008) and Smith (2005) state the importance of adopting a confident use of self, which links to both the practical application of self and understanding and articulating the theoretical justification for working in this way. This enables practitioners to have confidence in challenging risk aversion. In an evaluation of social pedagogical practice, Milligan (2011, p. 15) suggested that practitioners working within social pedagogy found a helpful framework on which to '"hang" the ideas and practices whilst defending an activity in terms of the developmental benefits rather than solely in terms of possible risks'.

While the values and overall approach of social pedagogy often appeal to practitioners, the challenge is often perceived as lacking the time, support or authority to pursue this approach. Within the context of risk, there is heightened pressure to remain within the procedural boundaries. The development of person-centred approaches which embed the principle of managing and minimising risk has therefore been helpful in supporting practitioners to embrace notions of choice and positive risk taking. Bates and Silberman (2007) introduced the concept of the Holy Grail to risk management. The model integrates the balance between *positive risk taking* around the values of autonomy and independence and a commitment to protection for the person and the community based on minimising harm. Bates and Silberman did not intend the Holy Grail to be a prescriptive tool but rather a list of criteria that an approach would have to fulfil:

1   Involvement of service users' and relatives' risk assessment
2   Positive and informed risk taking

3 Proportionality
4 Contextualising behaviour
5 Defensible decisions
6 Learning culture
7 Tolerable risks.

Employing many of the person-centred tools developed by Helen Sanderson (Sanderson and Lewis, 2012) and building on the Holy Grail criteria, Neill et al. (2008) developed a *positive person-centred approach to risk*. This built on the assumption that the underlying purpose of risk assessment should equally focus on the happiness of the person and their family as it should on their safety. Exploring some of the Holy Grail criteria will allow us to see the parallels with social pedagogical practice. Firstly, the criteria are focused on involving the individual and those that know them well at the centre of the process. The role of family, friends and supporters is to help understand how risk is framed for the individual from their perspective rather than from that of the service provider or the local authority. Secondly, the Holy Grail embraces a *strengths-based approach* to focus on the strengths, skills and gifts an individual possesses rather than weaknesses and deficits. Like the Diamond Model presented by Eichsteller and Holthoff (2011b, cited in Cameron and Moss, 2011b), there is a recognition that all human beings have potential and strengths. The identification of strengths is central to the utilisation of them in reaching goals balanced with maintaining safety. The identification of strengths is not the antithesis of identification of problems or risks. Instead, it is a large part of the solution (Graybeal, 2001). As this will be unique to all individuals, practitioners need to be able to think and respond creatively. Hatton (2013), drawing on ideas of social pedagogy across Europe, highlighted the importance of practitioners embracing creativity as part of their practice in the UK. In their *positive person-centred risk approach*, Neill et al. (2008) refer to the importance of a learning culture, as highlighted in the sixth criterion of the Holy Grail, to support positive risk taking with a deep emphasis on the use of reflection. They refer to the need to define core duties and understand one's *zone of judgement* and *creativity* in relation to risk. As discussed above, *learning* is a key component of social pedagogy both in terms of the professional and the individual but also in relation to developing a learning culture within organisations in order to support practitioners to be permitted and feel safe to employ creativity and judgement with integrity. Finally, Neill et al. (2008) encourage tolerable risks to be taken where the quality of life can be improved, as stated in the seventh criterion of the Holy Grail. As discussed earlier in relation to developing *risk competence*, the focus of the work emphasises supporting the individual to identify risks and learn to manage risk effectively to support well-being rather than removing risks to keep people safe.

Relationships and Working Alongside Risk

The use of self in social work practice is inextricably linked to a relationship-based practice. In Chapters 1 and 3 we explored the centrality of relationships within social pedagogy, supported through the application of Pestalozzi's Head, Heart and Hands model along with attention to concepts such as the Three Ps and the Relational Universe based upon one's *Haltung*, reflecting a profound respect for all individuals and a belief in their potential. The importance of relationships extends beyond the interaction between the practitioner and the individual to focus on the potential of relationships between individuals, their networks and the wider community. This is often referred to as relational practice whereby the relationship is recognised as a critical resource or tool in practice. Research with those accessing services and support has continued to reveal that the most important factor of the success of services provided by care professionals was the quality of their relationships (Beresford and Andrews, 2012; Center on the Developing Child at Harvard University, 2017). As the managing partner of The Innovation Unit, a programme working to promote better life endings, Gillinson (2017) calls for the creation of care systems where human relationships are given much higher priority. She highlighted the importance of making the quality of relationships a priority at every level – from leaders to frontline workers through organisational vision, service contracts, recruitment and accountability frameworks. In relation to risk, Gillinson urges a new balance between risk management and relational support by enabling social workers to do what they do best: building on strengths, employing empathy and creative, flexible support based on long-term solutions. From a social pedagogical perspective, an approach that recognises the multilayered potential of relationships in supporting the development of social competence, used in the way described above, supports the wider aims of social justice and the sustainability of well-being as opposed to a heavily regulated and procedural driven response to risk.

In Chapter 5, we referred to the concept of *meaningful belonging*. Rothuizen and Harbo (2017) referred to *bonding* and *bridging* whereby the practitioner enters into an *inclusive relationship* with the individual (being part of their everyday life). In turn, the experience of being part of an *inclusive relationship* can support their ability to enter *inclusive communities* and experience positive, inclusive relationships beyond this. Rothuizen and Harbo (2017) stressed the use of self in this process as being fundamental to the individual developing future positive interdependent relationships. The importance of supporting this process in relation to risk is clearly illustrated in the case of Steven Hoskins who was murdered in 2006. Steven had a learning disability and had been targeted by a group of individuals who exploited, degraded, brutally tortured and finally murdered him by leading him to and pushing him off a viaduct. In the Serious Case Review conducted by Flynn (2007), she highlighted poor practice in the failure for information to be shared appropriately, even though a number of concerns had been raised across agencies and services. The report also questioned the failure to investigate Steven's decision to terminate contact with adult social care given his vulnerability. He had been assessed by the existing Fair Access to Care criteria (DoH, 2002) as having a substantial need and therefore entitled to weekly social care visits. Finally, it was reported that Steven had spoken to an old friend shortly before he was murdered, excited to share his news of having his own bedsit, his dog and then revealed his exciting secret '*I am in a gang*'. In reading the report and testimonials from those who knew Steven, it was clear that he desperately wanted to feel part of a friendship group, particularly after his own relationship with his mother had deteriorated. The support being offered from social care fundamentally focused on help to carry out daily living tasks and support independent living. However, for Steven, it would appear the crucial support required was relational. As Rothuizen and Harbo (2017) suggest, individuals strive for a sense of *meaningful belonging*. Steven may well have benefited from a professional developing an *inclusive relationship* with him, getting to know his day-to-day life and modelling a positive, inclusive relationship. Imagine if the professional had been able to spend time with Steven and start the *bridging* stage of Rothuizen's model, helping him to connect with inclusive and positive communities. Instead, Steven had to navigate his own way around relationships and given his learning disability and obvious loneliness he could only engage in destructive relationships which bridged his step into a destructive community who eventually murdered him. Arguably Steven was failed at many levels, firstly the absence (at the time) of any specific legal duty relating to safeguarding; secondly the lack of coordination of support and emergency services but also the rigidity of social care systems that appear to perceive the development and utilisation of relational practice as a luxury, particularly at a time when resources become finite.

The importance of meaningful belonging and inclusive relationships can also be linked to social work practice with children and young people. Risk and risk management is the core focus of any contact with children and young people within the youth justice system. Here legislation tasks local authorities to tackle and reduce the offending behaviour of children and young people in their area whilst also providing protection to the public. Reduction in reoffending and risk management have become the key focus of practice within the youth justice system, driven by the modernisation and preventative agenda set in place by the New Labour government and enshrined in the Crime and Disorder Act (1998). Underpinning this ideological shift from welfare-led approaches to a more punitive and controlling focus are the evidence-based ideas of risk prediction and the *risk factors prevention paradigm* (Case, 2007). This paradigm developed a risk assessment tool that uses identified social, economic and statistical factors to assess the likelihood of an increase in risk behaviour. These factors are seen as the evidence base on which to set out a plan of intervention as part of a court order given to a young person with the aim of reducing offending and risk to the public and the young person.

The What Works agenda within the criminal justice system has identified affective factors in the reduction of reoffending but has given little if no consideration to what young people feel would have helped (Sapouna et al., 2011). In their study Larkins and Wainwright (2014, p. i) undertook participatory research activities with young people involved with the youth justice service, exploring their lived experience and what assisted them to reduce or stop reoffending and reduced risky behaviour. Unsurprisingly, the most important factor for these young people was their relationship with their Youth Offending Team (YOT) officer and the key element, that this relationship was respectful, empathic and supported them to engage, reflect and change. The second key finding was the importance of their YOT officer being actively involved with their families. Often the focus of youth justice work is with the young person and interventions take place within the YOT office and not within the family home or life world of the young person. The young people valued the YOT officers who took time to allow a young person to take the lead in helping them build or manage their relationships with their families as well as include their families in the contact they were having with the young person. But this also went further in being able to assist the young person to become engaged in meaningful activities within their communities and with regard to education, training and employment. The opportunity for the practitioner to become involved in the everyday life of the individual enables the possibility to build an inclusive relationship, referred to as the bonding element of Rothuizen and Harbo's (2017) model of *meaningful belonging*. As the young person built trust and self-confidence, they welcomed the practitioner in supporting them to develop positive connections with family and the wider community, the *bridging* element thus encouraging and facilitating the opportunity to engage with inclusive communities rather than the destructive ones that, in many cases, led them to entering the criminal justice system in the first place.

Conclusion

In this chapter we have explored the contentious notion of risk and how this can be understood and applied from a social pedagogical perspective. It would be naive to suggest that we can simply transfer European models of risk management to a UK context given the major differences in the way risk and welfare are understood across countries. It is however useful to reflect on these differences and recognise how conceptions of risk and welfare determine the way legislation, policy and practice are constructed in a particular setting. It is clear, however, that the adoption of social pedagogical approaches to risk requires extending interventions with young people and adults beyond a paternalistic framework to take greater account of ideas of rights, growth and opportunity. Smith (2012, p. 50) comments on social pedagogical literature that commonly refers to the *rich child* as opposed to the *child in need* conceived within a UK context. Similarly, we might consider what constitutes *rich adulthood* or a sense of *personhood* focusing on strengths and potentials rather than deficits. The concept of *risk competence* as described by Eichsteller and Holthoff (2009) calls for a different engagement with risk management which starts from an individual rather than service perspective, based on a strengths-based perspective and reference to the Life World Orientation model. It is one that fundamentally acknowledges the inextricable link between the risk activity and the individual and seeks solutions that emphasise benefits to well-being, opportunities and happiness as well as minimising harm. Importantly, it does not view risk as a universally negative construct and in need, therefore, of removing. Instead, the social pedagogical focus on learning is used to support individuals to identify risks and learn to manage them.

The social pedagogical approach to learning is a collaborative one. Learning is perhaps one of the less familiar concepts to the tradition of social work in the UK context and is more commonly understood within an educational framework. Social pedagogy is concerned with the educational dimension of social issues and the social dimension of educational aims. Therefore, from a social pedagogical perspective, working alongside risk calls for practitioners to embrace the notion of learning as discussed above in relation to the learning zone, making safeguarding personal and risk assessments with young people. This requires interventions to shift from procedural to relational approaches, in order to understand and individualise our responses and support. Smith (2012, p. 52) suggests that engagements based upon professionals as experts or supervisors must give way as pedagogues become 'co-constructors of meaning or fellow travellers in journeys of growth'.

The use of self and one's relationships in practice has been clearly stated throughout this book, reflecting its centrality within social pedagogy. The chapter has explored the specific relevance of relational practice within a risk context, highlighting the opportunities to support individuals to develop positive, sustainable relationships and healthy connections with communities, which inherently serve to protect individuals from a whole range of physical and emotional risks from abuse and exploitation through to loneliness, depression and self-neglect.

Finally, in this chapter, we must acknowledge the fact that many social workers already strive to and embrace many of the approaches identified when working alongside risk, despite the intrusion of risk averse systems and procedures dominating decision-making and practice. This collision of opposing agendas surrounding the promotion of well-being, choice and protection, articulated in legislation, including the Children Act (1989), the Mental Capacity Act (2005), the Care Act (2014) and the Human Rights Act (1998) to name a few, continues to challenge social workers seeking to adopt both a legal and ethical approach to their work. Smith (2012) stressed the importance of good leadership and organisational commitment to working alongside risk. Likewise, Spratt (2001) noted the importance of social workers having the permission to make changes to their practice. The opportunity and willingness, therefore, for practitioners and leaders to explore alternative philosophical and theoretical frameworks such as those offered from a social pedagogical perspective provide a useful basis to re-evaluate and reinvigorate social work practice.

Further Reading

Eichsteller, G. and Holthoff, S. (2017)*Towards a Pedagogic Conceptualisation of Risk.* www.thempra.org.uk/downloads/risk.pdf (accessed 24/7/18).

Neill, M., Allen, J., Woodhead, N., Reid, S., Irwin, L. and Sanderson, H. (2008) *A Positive Approach to Risk Requires Person Centred Thinking – A Think Local Act Personal Resource Paper.* www.thinklocalactpersonal.org.uk/_assets/Resources/Personalisation/Personalisation_advice/A_Person_Centred_Approach_to_Risk.pdf (accessed 2/8/18).

CONCLUSION

LOWIS CHARFE AND ALI GARDNER

At the time of writing this book, social pedagogy was an emerging concept in the UK, as practitioners and scholars became interested in the considerable importance it held across the European mainland. The book, therefore, provides an historical background of the academic and practice-based developments of social pedagogy in order to support the reader in exploring the potential application of social pedagogy within a UK context. In reviewing these developments, the reader will note some examples of social pedagogy being embedded within policy and practice in the UK, providing evidence of the positive contribution and alignment it has with social work.

The book sets out to define social pedagogy and locates the focus on and connection between social care and education. It introduces a number of social pedagogical concepts, including *Haltung*, Life World Orientation, relational practice and the Common Third, which allow the reader to engage with the fundamental ethical orientation of this approach. For those working in social work and social care, the ideas explored in this book may well resonate with your own practice and, more importantly, your understanding of why you entered the profession in the first place.

Throughout the book, the authors have aimed to make specific links with the current legislative and policy agendas in order to explore both the opportunities and threats in applying social pedagogical practice in relation to both child and adult social work. As governments continue to grapple with balancing competing imperatives around promoting independence and safeguarding individuals at a time of increasing austerity, the authors explore the potential contribution of social pedagogy. Principally, the approach requires a paradigmatic shift in the practitioner's understanding of their role and purpose in working alongside individuals. The book explores the ways in which *relationship-based* and *relational social work* can occupy a central position in practice thus challenging some of the process-driven mechanisms that have increasingly dominated the profession in recent years. Likewise, the book explores the importance of collaborative learning and creativity with the individuals that we work alongside in order to acknowledge and promote the expertise of individuals and enhance meaningful well-being and growth.

Social pedagogy essentially concentrates on the individual, their families, their communities and wider society, viewing the inextricable link that exists between them. A focus of the book, therefore, has been to explore the wide-ranging roles practitioners, agencies and governments must play in promoting opportunities to build inclusive relationships and communities offering a sense of belonging to individuals. This requires flexible rather than fragmented systems and support, which are person-centred, at every point of intervention, whether that be supporting individuals in accessing daily living support or safeguarding situations with high levels of risk and complexity. In Chapter 7, the contentious issues surrounding risk and risk management are explored from a social pedagogical perspective. In that chapter, we reflect on the risk averse contexts within which social work takes place and consider the values, knowledge, skills and support that are required to embed a *risk competent* approach to working with individuals and their families.

Fundamentally, the book has attempted to introduce the key tenets of social pedagogy and demonstrate their relevance and alignment to social work values and practice. The book offers an opportunity to explore alternative philosophical and theoretical frameworks which can complement and support social care practitioners in their working alongside individuals, families and their communities.

REFERENCES

Adams, E. and Ingham, S. (1998) *Changing Places: Children's Participation in Environmental Planning*. London: The Children's Society.

Alanen, L. (1988) Rethinking childhood. *Acta Sociologica 31*(1): 53–67.

American Montessori Society (2018) Maria Montessori biography. Available at: https://amshq.org/Montessori-Education/History-of-Montessori-Education/Biography-of-Maria-Montessori (accessed 2 July 2018).

Anderson, S. (2008) *Later Life Learning: A Review of the Literature*. London: Association for Education and Ageing.

Asquith, S. (2006) *The Kilbrandon Report: Children and Young Persons Scotland*. Edinburgh: HMSO.

Asquith, S., Clark, C. and Waterhouse, L. (2005) *The Role of the Social Worker in the 21st Century: A Literature Review*. Edinburgh: Scottish Government.

Badham, B. and Wade, H. (2005) *Hear by Right* (rev. edn). The National Youth Agency, Local Government Association: Blackburn.

Bandura, A. (1997) *Self-Efficacy*. New York: W.H. Freeman and Company.

Barnes, C. and Mercer, G. (2010) *Exploring Disability* (2nd edn). Cambridge: Polity Press.

BASW (British Association of Social Workers) (2012) *Code of Ethics*. London: BASW.

Bates, P. and Silberman, W. (2007) *Modelling Risk Management in Inclusive Settings*. London: National Development Team. Available at: www.ndt.org.uk/docsN/ET_SIrisk.pdf (accessed 1 August 2018).

Bengtsson, E.E, Chamberlain, C., Crimmens, D. and Stanley, J. (2008) *Introducing Social Pedagogy into Residential Child Care in England*. Available at: www.thetcj.org/wp-content/uploads/2008/03/introducing-sp-into-rcc-in-england-final-reportfeb2008.pdf.

Beresford, P. and Andrews, E. (2012) *Caring for Our Future: What Service Users Say*. Programme Paper York: Joseph Rowntree Foundation.

Bessell, A.G. (2001) Children surviving cancer: Psychological adjustment, quality of life, and school experiences. *Exceptional Children 67*(3): 345–59.

Biggeri, B., Ballet, J. and Comim, F. (2011) *Children and the Capability Approach*. Basingstoke: Palgrave Macmillan.

Bilson, A. and Martin, E.C.K. (2016) Referrals and child protection in England: One in five children referred to Children's Services and one in nineteen investigated before the age of five, *The British Journal of Social Work 47*(3): 793–811. Available at: https://doi.org/10.1093/bjsw/bcw054.

Bilson, A., Featherstone, B. and Martin, K. (2017) How child protection's 'investigative turn' impacts on poor and deprived communities. *Family Law 47*: 316–19.

Blyth, C. and Gardner, A. (2007) 'We're not asking for anything special': Direct payments and carers of disabled children. *Disability and Society 22*(3): 235–49.

Boyden, J. (2003) Children under fire: Challenging assumptions about children's resilience. *Children, Youth and Environments 13*(1): 1–29.

Boyden, J. and Ennew, J. (1997) *Children in Focus – A Manual for Participatory Research*. Sweden: Save The Children.

Brisenden, S. (1986) Independent living and the medical model of disability. *Journal of Disability, Handicap and Society* 1(2): 173–8.

British Association of Social Work (2018) *Professional Capability Framework*. Available at: www.basw.co.uk/system/files/resources/Detailed%20level%20descriptors%20for%20 all%20domains%20wi%20digital%20aug8.pdfers

Brühlmeier, A. (2010) *Head Heart and Hand: Education in the Spirit of Pestalozzi*. Cambridge: Open Book Publishers.

Cameron, C. (2017) Social pedagogy: The approach that intertwines well-being and learning. Available at: https://ioelondonblog.wordpress.com/2017/02/28/social-pedagogy-the-approach-that-intertwines-well-being-and-learning/

Cameron, C. and Moss, P. (eds) (2011a) *Social Pedagogy and Working with Children and Young People*. London: Jessica Kingsley.

Cameron, C. and Moss, P. (2011b) Social pedagogy: Current understandings and opportunities. In Cameron, C. and Moss, P. (eds) *Social Pedagogy and Working with Children and Young People*. London: Jessica Kingsley.

Cameron, C., Petrie, P., Wigfall, V., Kleipoedszuz, S. and Jasper, A. (2011) *Final Report of the Social Pedagogy Pilot Programme: Development and Implementation*. London: Thomas Coram Research Unit, Institute of Education, University of London.

Carter, A. and Eichsteller, G. (2017) Cultivating a Relational Universe. *Therapeutic Care Journal*. Available at: www.thetcj.org/in-residence-articles/cultivating-relational-universe-andy-carter-gabriel-eichsteller (accessed 24 July 2018).

Case, S. (2007) Questioning the 'evidence' of risk that underpins evidence-led youth justice interventions. *Youth Justice* 7(2): 91–105.

Cavadino, M. and Dignan, J. (2006) *The Penal System: An Introduction*. London: Sage.

Cavadino, M., Dignan, J. and Anspach, D. (2006) *Penal Systems: A Comparative Approach*. London: SAGE Publishers.

Center on the Developing Child at Harvard University (2017) Three Principles to Improve Outcomes for Children aand Families. Available at https://developingchild.harvard.edu/resources/three-early-childhood-development-principles-improve-child-family-outcomes/

Chambers, H. and Petrie, P. (2009) *A Learning Framework for Artist Pedagogues*. London: Creativity, Culture and Education and National Children's Bureau.

Cooke, B and Kothari, U. (2004) *Participation: The New Tyranny*. London: Palgrave.

Cooper, A. (2012) The self in social work practice: Uses and abuses. Paper presented at the CSWP/Essex University day conference 'How to do Relationship-based Social Work', Southend, 13 January. Available at: www.cfswp. org/education/paper.php?s...self-in-socialwork-practice-uses-and-abuses/html.

Cottam, H. (2008) *Beveridge 4.0*. London: Participle Limited.

Cottam, H. (2018) *Radical Help: How We Can Remake the Relationships Between Us and Revolutionise the Welfare State*. London: Virago.

Cousseé, F., Bradt, L., Roose, R. and Bouverne-De Bie, M. (2010) The emerging social pedagogical paradigm in UK child and youth care: Deus ex machina or walking the beaten path? *British Journal of Social Work* 40(3): 789–805.

Coyne, I., McNamara, N., Healy, M., Gower, C., Sarkar, M. and McNicholas, F. (2015) Adolescents' and parents' views of Child and Adolescent Mental Health Services (CAMHS) in Ireland. *Journal of Psychiatric and Mental Health Nursing* 22(8): 561–9.

Creative Commons (2012) *Participation Models Citizens, Youth, Online: A Chase through the Maze* (2nd edn). Available at: www.nonformality.org/participation-models (accessed 12 May 2018).

Cree, V. and Wallace, S. (2005) Risk and protection. In Adams, R., Dominelli, L. and Payne, M. (eds) *Social Work Futures*. Basingstoke: Palgrave Macmillan. pp. 115–27.

Cregan, K. and Cuthbert, D. (2014) *Global Childhoods: Issues and Debates*. London: Sage.

Cunningham, J. and Cunningham, S. (2014) *Sociology and Social Work*. London: Sage/Learning Matters.

Day, C. (2008) Children and young people's involvement and participation in mental health care. *Child and Adolescent Mental Health 13*(1): 2–8.

Derbyshire County Council (2017) Derbyshire County Council: Using 'creative mentoring' to support looked after children. Available at: www.local.gov.uk/derbyshire-county-council-using-creative-mentoring-support-looked-after-children (accessed 24 November 2017).

DfE (Department for Education) (2010) *Independent Reviewing Officers Handbook*. Available at: https://assets.publishing.service.gov.uk/government/uploads/system/uploads/attachment_data/file/337568/iro_statutory_guidance_iros_and_las_march_2010_tagged.pdf (accessed 10 June 2018).

DfE (Department for Education) (2018a) *Knowledge and Skills Statement for Child and Family Practitioners*. Available at: https://assets.publishing.service.gov.uk/government/uploads/system/uploads/attachment_data/file/691575/Knowledge_and_skills_statement_for_child_and_family_practitioners.pdf (accessed 17 May 2018).

DfE (Department for Education) (2018b) *Working Together to Safeguard Children: Statutory Guidance on Interagency Work to Safeguard and Promote the Welfare of Children*. London: DfE.

Department for Education and Skills (2007) *Care Matters: Time for Change*. Available at: www.gov.uk/government/publications/care-matters-time-for-change.

DoH (Department of Health) (2002) *Fair Access to Care Services: Guidance and Eligibility Criteria for Adult Social Care*. London: DoH.

DoH (Department of Health) (2007) *Putting People First : A Shared Vision and Commitment to the Transformation of Adult Social Care*. London: Department of Health.

DoH (Department of Health) (2015a) *Code of Practice (2015) Mental Health Act (1983)*. London: TSO.

DoH (Department of Health) (2015b) *Knowledge and Skills Statement for Social Workers in Adult Services*. Available at: https://assets.publishing.service.gov.uk/government/uploads/system/uploads/attachment_data/file/411957/KSS.pdf.

DoH (Department of Health) (2017) *You're Welcome Pilot Revised 2017*. Available at: www.gov.uk/government/publications/quality-criteria-for-young-people-friendly-health-services (accessed 10 June 2018).

DoH (Department of Health) (2018) *Care and Support Statutory Guidance*, August 2017. London: DoH.

Doyle, M. and Smith, M. (2007) Jean-Jacques Rousseau on education. *The Encyclopaedia of Informal Education*. Available at: www.infed.org/thinkers/et-rous.htm (last update 7 January 2013).

Eichsteller, G. (2010) The notion of 'Haltung' in social pedagogy. *Children Webmag*. Available at: www.childrenwebmag.com/articles/social-pedagogy/the-notion-of-'haltung-in-social-pedagogy.

Eichsteller, G. (2017) Janusz Korczak: His legacy and its relevance for children's rights. In Kilkelly, U. and Lundy, L. (eds) *Children's Rights: The Library of Essays on Family Rights*. Abingdon: Routledge.

Eichsteller, G. and Holthoff, S. (2009) Risk competence: Towards a pedagogic conceptualisation of risk. *Children Webmag 9*. Available at: www.thempra.org.uk/downloads/risk.pdf (accessed 2 January 2019).

Eichsteller, G. and Holthoff, S. (2011a) Conceptual foundations of social pedagogy: A transnational perspective from Germany. In Cameron, C. and Moss, P. (eds) *Social Pedagogy and Working with Children and Young People*. London: Jessica Kingsley.

Eichsteller, G. and Holthoff, S. (2011b) Social pedagogy as an ethical orientation towards working with people – historical perspectives. *Children Australia 36*(4): 176–86.

Eichsteller, G. and Holthoff, S. (2012) The art of being a social pedagogue: Developing cultural change in children's homes in Essex. *International Journal of Social Pedagogy 1*(1): 30–46.

Eichsteller, G. and Holthoff, S. (2017) *Towards a Pedagogic Conceptualisation of Risk*. Available at: www.thempra.org.uk/downloads/risk.pdf (accessed 24 July 2018).

Eichsteller, G., Holthoff, S. and Kemp, R. (2014) *Social Pedagogy Training Pack*. ThemPra Social Pedagogy Community Interest Company.

Featherstone, B., Broadhurst, K., and Holt, K. (2012a). Thinking systemically-thinking politically: Building strong partnerships with children and families in the context of rising inequality. *British Journal of Social Work 42*(4): 618–33.

Featherstone, B., Morris, K., Gray, M., Midgley, J. and Webb, S.A. (2012b) *Feminist Ethics of Care The SAGE Handbook of Social Work*. London: Sage.

Featherstone, B., Morris, K. and White, S. (2014) A marriage made in hell. Early intervention meets child protection. *The British Journal of Social Work 44*(7): 1735–49.

Feilberg, F. (2008) *Use of Self in Residential Child Care*. Residence series No. 8, May. Glasgow: Scottish Institute for Residential Child Care. Available at: www.sircc.org.uk/sites/default/files/In_Residence_8.pdf (accessed 1 August 2018).

Ferguson, I. (2008) *Reclaiming Social Work: Challenging Neoliberalism and Promoting Social Justice*. London: Sage.

Ferguson, I. (2012) Personalisation, social justice and social work: a reply to Simon Duffy. *Journal of Social Work Practice 26*(1): 55–73.

Ferguson, I. and Woodward, R. (2009) *Radical Social Work in Practice: Making a Difference*. Bristol: The Policy Press.

Flynn, M. (2007) *Serious Case Review Report: The Murder of Steven Hoskins*. Cornwall: Cornwall Adult Protection Committee.

Freire, P. (1970) *Pedagogy of the Oppressed*. London: Penguin.

Freire, P. (1996) *Pedagogy of the Oppressed* (2nd edn). London: Penguin.

Freire, P. (2001) *Pedagogy of Freedom: Ethics, Democracy and Civic Courage*. Oxford: Rowman and Littlefield.

Frith, E. (2016) *Progress and Challenges in the Transformation of Children and Young People's Mental Health Care: A Report of the Education Policy Institute's Mental Health Commission*. London: Education Policy Institute.

Frost, N. and Parton, N. (2009) *Understanding Children's Social Care: Politics, Policy and Practice*. London: SAGE.

Gallagher, M. (2008) Foucault, power and participation. *International Journal of Children's Rights 16*(3): 395–406.

Gardner, A. (2014) *Personalisation and Social Work* (2nd edn). Exeter: Learning Matters.

Gerhardt, H. (1994) Paulo Freire. In Morsy, Z. (ed.) *Thinkers on Education 2 (Prospects)*. Paris: UNESCO. Available at: www.ibe.unesco.org/publications/ThinkersPdf/grundtve.pdf.

Gillinson, S. (2017) Why relationships are key to good social work. Available at: www.theguardian.com/social-care-network/2017/mar/21/why-relationships-are-key-to-good-social-work (accessed 1 August 2018).

Godden, N.J. (2017) The love ethic: A radical theory for social work practice. *Journal of Australian Social Work 70*(4): 405–46.

Goldson, B. and Muncie, J. (eds) (2011) *Critical Anatomy: Towards a Principled Youth Justice in Youth Crime and Justice*. London: Sage.

Goldson, B and Muncie, J (eds) (2015) *Youth Crime and Justice* (2nd edn). London: Sage.

Graybeal, C. (2001) Strengths-based social work assessment: Transforming the dominant paradigm. *Families in Society: The Journal of Contemporary Human Services 82*(3): 233–42.

Greenaway, R. (1992) Reviewing by doing. *Journal of Adventure Education and Outdoor Leadership*. Available at: www.reviewing.co.uk/articles/2rbd.htm#4stage (accessed 25 July 2018).

Grundwald, K. and Thiersch, H. (2009) The concept of the 'Lifeworld Orientation' for social work social care. *Journal of Social Work Practice 23*(2): 131–46.

Hadi, J. (2018) Dreaming of new horizons: Unaccompanied children and the Common Third. Available at: https://medium.com/@jameelhadi/dreaming-of-new-horizons-unaccompanied-children-and-the-common-third-a2f06d9b2759 (accessed 8 August 2018).

Hafford-Letchfield, T. (2010) Opportunities of older people using social care services. *The British Journal of Social Work 40*(2): 496–512.

Hämäläinen, J. (2003) The concept of social policy in the field of social work. *Journal of Social Work 3*(1): 69–80.

Harman, C. (2008) *A People's History of the World: From the Stone Age to the New Millennium*. London: Verso.

Hart, R.A. (1992) *Children's Participation from Tokenism to Citizenship*. Florence: UNICEF International Child Development Centre.

Hart, R.A. (2008) Stepping back from 'The Ladder': Reflections on a Model of Participatory Work with children. In Reid, A., Jenson, B.B., Nikel, J. and Simovisha, V. (eds) *Participation and Learning*. Dortrecht: Springer.

Hatton, K. (2013) *Social Pedagogy in the UK: Theory and Practice*. Lyme Regis: Russell House Publishing.

Hayes, D. (2017) Proximity, pain and state punishment. *Punishment and Society 20*(2): 235–54.

Hazel, N. (2008) *A Cross-national Comparison of Youth Justice*. London: Youth Justice Board.

HCPC (Health and Care Professions Council) (2017) *Standards of Proficiency: Social Workers in England*. Available at: www.hcpc-uk.org/globalassets/resources/standards/standards-of-proficiency---social-workers-in-england.pdf (accessed 1 June 2018).

Holmes, R. (2014) *Eleanor Marx: A Life*. London: Bloomsbury Publishing.

House of Commons (2018) *Adult Social Care Funding (England)*. London: House of Commons Library.

Howe, D. (1998) Relationship-based thinking and practice in social work. *Journal of Social Work Practice 16*(2): 45–56.

Ingram, R. (2013) Locating emotional intelligence at the heart of social work practice. *British Journal of Social Work 43*(5): 987–1004.

Invernissi, A. and Williams, J. (2009) *The Human Rights of Children: From Visions to Implementation*. Abingdon: Routledge.

Investing in Children (2013) Available at: www.investinginchildren.net (accessed 10 June 2018).

Jacaranda (2015) *Social Pedagogy: An Invitation*. London: Jacaranda Development.

Jackson, N. and Burgess, H. (2005) *Creativity in Social Work and Social Education: Disciplinary Perspectives on Creativity in Higher Education*. A Working Paper. The Higher Education Academy. Available at: www.creativeacademic.uk/uploads/1/3/5/4/13542890/creativity_in_social_work.pdf (accessed 24 July 2018).

James, A. and Prout, A. (1990) *Constructing and Reconstructing Childhood*. Basingstoke: Falmer Press.

James, A., Jenks, C. and Prout, A. (1998) *Theorizing Childhood*. Basingstoke: Palgrave MacMillan.

Jappe, E. (2010) The 3 Ps. Available at: http://10rs1gruppe6.blogspot.com/2010/09/de-3-per.html (accessed 24 July 2018).

Jones, S. (2009) *Critical Learning for Social Work Students*. Exeter: Learning Matters.

Jones, P. and Walker, G. (2011) *Children's Rights in Practice*. London: Sage.

Kahl, R. (2001) Lernen ist Vorfreude aut sich selbst. *Padogigik 1*: 110–13.

Kaushik, A. (2017) Use of self in social work: Rhetoric or reality. *Journal of Social Work Values and Ethics 14*(1): 1–21.

Keay, D. (1987) Interview for *Women's Own* ('No such thing as society'). Available at: www.margaretthatcher.org/document/106689 (accessed17 May 2018).

Keddell, E. (2018) The vulnerable child in neoliberal contexts: the constructions of children in the Aotearoa New Zealand child protection reforms. *Childhood 25*(1): 93–108.

Kelly, P. (2016) *Creative Mentoring with Children in Care: An Enhanced Review*. Available at: www.derbyshire.gov.uk/site-elements/documents/pdf/social-health/children-and-families/children-we-look-after/the-virtual-school/creative-mentoring-an-enhanced-review.pdf.

Kemshall, H. (2002) *Risk, Social Policy and Welfare*. Milton Keynes: Open University Press.

Kettle, M. and Jackson, S. (2017) Revisiting the rule of optimism. *The British Journal of Social Work 47*(6): 1624–40.

Kirby, P., Lanyon, C., Cronin, K. and Sinclair, R. (2003) *Building a Culture of Participation: Involving Children and Young People in Policy, Service Planning, Delivery and Evaluation*. London: DfES.

Korczak, J. (2007) *Loving Every Child – Wisdom for Parents*, edited by S. Joseph. Chapel Hill, NC: Alogonquin Books.

Kornbeck, J. (2009) 'Important but widely misunderstood': The problem of defining social pedagogy in Europe. In Kornbeck, J. and Jensen, N. (eds) *The Diversity of Social Pedagogy in Europe*. Bremen: Europaischer Hochschulverlag.

Laird, S. (2010) *Practical Social Work Law: Analysing Court Cases and Inquiries*. Harlow: Pearson Education.

Lansdown, G. (2004) Criteria for the evaluation of children's participation in programming. In Bernard van Leer Foundation (ed.) *Early Childhood Matters*. The Hague: Bernard van Leer Foundation.

Lansdown, G. (2011) *Every Child's Right to be Heard: A Resource Guide on the UN Committee on the Rights of the Child General Comment No 12*. London: Save the Children.

Lansdown, G. and O'Kane, C. (2014) *A Toolkit for Monitoring and Evaluating Children's Participation*. London: Save the Children.

Larkins, C. and Wainwright, J. (2014) *'Just Putting Me on the Right Track': Young People's Perspectives on What Helps Them Stop Offending*. Project Report. Preston: University of Central Lancashire.

Lawson, M. (1994) Nikolay Grundtvig. In Morsy, Z. (ed.) *Thinkers on Education 2 (Prospects)*. Paris: UNESCO. Available at: www.ibe.unesco.org/sites/default/files/grundtve.pdf.

Lewowicki, T. (1997) Janusz Korczak. In Morsy, Z. (ed.) *Thinkers on Education*, Vol. 3. Paris: UNESCO. Available at: www.ibe.unesco.org/publications/ThinkersPdf/korczaks.pdf.

Lihme, B. (1988) *Socialpædagogikken for born og unge: et debatoplæg med særligt henblik pa døgninstitutionen*. Holte: Scopol.

Lorenz, W. (2004) Towards a European paradigm of social work: Studies in the history of modes of social work and social policy in Europe. Doctor of Philosophy Thesis, Technical University of Dresden.

Malaguzzi, L. (1993) History, ideas and basic philosophy. In Edwards, C., Gandini, L. and Forman, G. (eds) *The Hundred Languages Children: The Reggio Emilia Approach to Early Childhood Education*. Norwood, NJ: Ablex.

Mannion, G. (2007) Going spatial, going relational: Why 'listening to children' and children's participation needs reframing. *Discourse: Studies in the Cultural Politics of Education 28*(3): 405–20.

Marsh, P. and Doel, M. (2005) *The Task-centred Book*. Abingdon: Routledge.

McAra, L. (2012) Models of youth justice. In Smith, D. (ed.) *A New Response to Youth Crime*. Abingdon: Routledge.

McDermid, S., Holmes, L., Ghate, D., Blackmore, J. and Baker, C. (2016) *The Evaluation of Head, Heart and Hands: Introducing Social Pedagogy into UK Foster Care*. Loughborough: The Centre for Child and Family Research, Loughborough University, and the Colebrooke Centre for Evidence and Implementation.

Meyer, J.H.F. and Land, R. (2006) *Overcoming Barriers to Student Understanding: Threshold Concepts and Troublesome Knowledge*. New York: Routledge.

Milligan, I. (2011) Resisting risk-averse practice: The contribution of social pedagogy. *Children Australia 36*(4): 207–13.

Morgan, H. (2012) The social model of disability as a threshold concept: Troublesome knowledge and liminal spaces in social work education. *Social Work Education: The International Journal 31*(2): 215–26.

Morris, J. (2004) Independent living and community care: A disempowering framework. *Disability and Society 19*(5): 427–42.

Morris, T., Anderson, Y. and Nixon, B. (2009) New ways of working in Child and Adolescent Mental Helath Services – 'Keep the baby but throw out the bath water'. *The Journal of Mental Health Training, Education and Practice 4*(3): 10–14.

Mührel, E. (2008) *Verstehen und Achten. Philosophische Reflexionen zur professionellen Haltung in der Sozialen Arbeit*. Essen: Die Blaue Eule.

Muncie, J. and Goldson, B. (2006) *Comparative Youth Justice*. London: Sage.

Munro, E.R. (2011) *Munro Review of Child Protection: A Child Centred System*. Norwich: TSO.

NASW (National Association of Social Workers) (2011) *Code of Ethics of the National Association of Social Workers*. Available at: https://socialwork.utexas.edu/dl/files/academic-programs/other/nasw-code-of-ethics.pdf (accessed 8 August 2017).

Needham, C. and Glasby, J. (2014) *Debates in Personalisation*. Bristol: Policy Press.

Neill, M., Allen, J., Woodhead, N., Reid, S., Irwin, L. and Sanderson, H. (2008) *A Positive Approach to Risk Requires Person Centred Thinking – A Think Local Act Personal Resource Paper*. Available at: www.thinklocalactpersonal.org.uk/_assets/Resources/Personalisation/Personalisation_advice/A_Person_Centred_Approach_to_Risk.pdf (accessed 2 August 2018).

NFER (National Foundation for Educational Research) (2006) *The Longer Term Impact of Creative Partnerships on the Attainment of Young People*. A report by NFER. Available at: www.creativitycultureeducation.org/publication/the-longer-term-impact-of-creative-partnerships-on-the-attainment-of-young-people/ (accessed 24 July 2018).

Oliver, M. (2009) *Understanding Disability: From Theory to Practice*. London: Palgrave Macmillan.

Oxford English Dictionary (2018) Available at: https://en.oxforddictionaries.com/definition/social (accessed 9 January 2018).

Participation Works (2007) *How to Safeguard Children and Young People*. London: National Children's Bureau.

Percy-Smith, B. and Thomas, N. (2010) *A Handbook of Children and Young People's Participation Perspectives from Theory and Practice*. Abingdon: Routledge.

Petrie, P. (2006) Nineteenth-century understanding of care work. In Boddy, J., Cameron, C. and Moss, P. (eds) *Care Work: Present and Future*. Abingdon: Routledge.

Petrie, P. (2011) *Communication Skills for Working with Children and Young People: Introducing Social Pedagogy* (3rd edn). London: Jessica Kingsley Publishers.

Petrie, P. (2013) Social pedagogy in the UK: Gaining a firm foothold? *Education Policy Analysis Archives/Archivos Analíticos de Políticas Educativas* 21: 37.

Qvortrup, J., Bardy, M., Sgritta, G. and Wintersberger, H. (eds) (1994) *Childhood Matters: Social Theory, Practice and Politics*. Aldershot: Avebury.

Richter, J., Halliday, S., Grømer, L.I. and Dybdahl, R. (2009) User and care involvement in Child and Adolescent Mental Health Services: A Norwegian staff perspective. *Administration and Policy in Mental Health and Mental Health Services Research* 36: 265–77.

Robinson, K. (2006) *Do Schools Kill Creativity?* Available at: www.ted.com/speakers/sir_ken_robinson.

Robinson, K (2011) *Out of Our Minds: Learning to be Creative*. London: John Wiley.

Rogers, C. (1951) *Client Centred Therapy*. Boston: Houghton Mifflin.

Rogers, C. (1995) *Client-Centred Therapy: Its Current Practice, Implications and Theory*. London: Constable and Robinson.

Röhrs, H. (1994) Maria Montessori. In Morsy, Z. (ed.) *Thinkers on Education*, Vol. 3. Paris: UNESCO.

Rothuizen, J.J. and Harbo, L.J. (2017) Social pedagogy: An approach without fixed recipes. *International Journal of Social Pedagogy* 6(1): 6–28.

Ruch, G. (2005) Relationship-based practice and reflective practice: Holistic approaches to contemporary child care social work. *Child and Family Social Work* 10(2): 111–23.

Ruch, G., Turney, D. and Ward, A. (2010) *Relationship Based Social Work: Getting to the Heart of Practice*. London: Jessica Kingsley.

Russell, C. (2011) Pulling back from the edge: An asset-based approach to ageing well. *Working with Older People* 15(3): 96–105.

Rutherford, A. (1992) *Growing Out of Crime: The New Era*. Winchester: Waterside Press.

Saleeby, D. (ed.) (2006) *The Strengths Perspective in Social Work Practice* (4th edn). Boston: Allyn and Bacon.

Sanderson, H. (2000) *Person Centred Planning: Key Features and Approaches*. York: Joseph Rowntree Foundation.

Sanderson, H. and Lewis, J. (2012) *A Practical Guide to Delivering Personalisation: Person Centred Practice in Health and Social Care*. London: Jessica Kingsley.

Sapouna, M., Bisset, C. and Conlong, A.M. (2011) *What Works to Reduce Reoffending: A Review of the Literature*. Edinburgh: Scottish Government. Available at: www.scotland.gov.uk/Topics/Justice/public-safety/offender-management (accessed 2 August 2017).

Schon, D. (2016) *The Reflective Practitioner: How Professionals Think in Action*. Abingdon: Routledge.

Schugurensky, D. (2014) Social pedagogy and critical theory: A conversation with Hans Thiersch. *International Journal of Social Pedagogy* 3(1): 4–14.

Schwartz, I. (2001) Socialpædagogik og anbragte børn (1st edn). Copenhagen: Gyldendalske Boghandel, Nordisk Forlag.

Schwartz, R., Estein, O., Komaroff, J., Lamb, J., Myers, M., Stewart, J., Vacaflor, L. and Park, M. (2013) Mental health consumers and providers dialogue in an institutional setting: A participatory approach to promoting recovery-oriented care. *Psychiatric Rehabilitation Journal* 36(2): 113–15.

Scott, D. and Codd, H. (2010) *Controversial Issues in Prisons*. Berkshire: Open University Press.

Shier, H. (2001) Pathways to participation: Openings opportunities and obligations. *Children and Society* 15(2): 107–17.

Sinclair, R. (2004) Participation in practice: Making it meaningful, effective and sustainable. *Children and Society* 18(2): 110–16.

Smale, G., Tuson, G., Biehal, N. and Marsh, P. (1993) *Empowerment, Assessment, Care Management and the Skilled Worker*. London: NISW/HMSO.

Smith, M.K. (2002) Paulo Freire and informal education. *The Encyclopaedia of Informal Education*. Available at: http://infed.org/mobi/paulo-freire-dialogue-praxis-and-education/ (accessed 2 January 2019).

Smith, M.K. (2009a) Social pedagogy. *The Encyclopaedia of Informal Education*. Available at: http://infed.org/mobi/social-pedagogy-the-development-of-theory-and-practice/ (accessed 18 May 2018).

Smith, M. (2009b) *Rethinking Residential Child Care: Positive Perspectives*. Bristol: The Policy Press.

Smith, M. (2009c) Johann Heinrich Pestalozzi: Pedagogy, education and social justice. *The Encyclopaedia of Informal Education*. Available at: http://infed.org/mobi/johann-heinrich-pestalozzi-pedagogy-education-and-social-justice/ (accessed 20 June 2018).

Smith, M.K. (2011) N. F. S. Grundtvig, folk high schools and popular education. *The Encyclopaedia of Informal Education*. Available at: http://infed.org/mobi/n-f-s-grundtvig-folk-high-schools-and-popular-education/ (accessed 20 June 2018).

Smith, M. (2012) Social pedagogy from a Scottish perspective. *International Journal of Social Pedagogy* 1(1): 46–55.

Smith, M. (2014) Relationships. *Good Enough Caring Journal 16*.

Smith, M. and Whyte, B. (2008) Social education and social pedagogy: Reclaiming a Scottish tradition in social work. *European Journal of Social Work* 11(1): 15–28.

Smith, R. (2005) *Values and Practice in Children's Services*. Basingstoke: Palgrave Macmillan.

SPPA (Social Pedagogy Professional Association) (2017) *Social Pedagogy Professional Standards*. Available at: www.sppa-uk.org/governance/social-pedagogy-standards/ (accessed 14 June 2018).

Spratt, T. (2001) The influence of child protection orientation in child welfare practice. *The British Journal of Social Work 31*(6): 933–54.

St Christopher's Fellowship (2017) Social pedagogy: Finding the diamond. Available at: www.stchris.org.uk/services/st-christophers-approach/social-pedagogy.aspx.

Stephens, P. (2013) *Social Pedagogy: Heart and Head*. Studies in Comparative Social Pedagogies and International Social Work and Social Policy, Vol. XXIV. Bremen: Europaischer Hochschulverlag.

Storø, J. (2013) *Practical Social Pedagogy: Theories, Values and Tools for Working with Children and Young People*. Bristol: The Policy Press.

The Fostering Network (2011) *Head, Hands and Heart. Bringing up Children in Foster Care: A Social Pedagogic Approach: Funding Proposal*. London: The Fostering Network.

The Fostering Network (2017) Head, heart, hands. Available at: www.thefosteringnetwork.org.uk/policy-practice/projects-and-programmes/head-heart-hands.

ThemPra (2017a) The Learning Zone Model. Available at: www.thempra.org.uk/social-pedagogy/key-concepts-in-social-pedagogy/the-learning-zone-model/ (accessed 2 January 2019).

ThemPra (2017b) Social pedagogy. Available at: www.thempra.org.uk/social-pedagogy/.

ThemPra (2017c) The Common Third. Available at: www.thempra.org.uk/social-pedagogy/key-concepts-in-social-pedagogy/the-common-third/.

ThemPra (2017d) The Relational Universe. Available at: www.thempra.org.uk/social-pedagogy/key-concepts-in-social-pedagogy/relational-universe/.

ThemPra (2018) Haltung in social pedagogy. Available at: www.thempra.org.uk/social-pedagogy/key-concepts-in-social-pedagogy/haltung-in-social-pedagogy/ (accessed 10 November 2016).

Thomas, N. (2005) *Social Work with Young People in Care: Looking after Children in Theory and Practice*. Basingstoke: Palgrave Macmillan.

Thomas, N. (2007) Towards a theory of children's participation. *International Journal of Children's Rights 15*(2): 199–218.

Thompson, S. (2016) Promoting reciprocity in old age: A social work challenge. *Practice 28*(5): 341–55.

Treseder (1997) cited in Creative Commons, 2012.

Trevithick, P. (2003) Effective relationship-based practice: A theoretical exploration. *Journal of Social Work Practice 17*(2): 163–76.

Trevithick, P. (2014a) Humanising managerialism: Reclaiming emotional reasoning, intuition, the relationship, and knowledge and skills in social work. *Journal of Social Work Practice 28*(3): 287–311.

Trevithick, P. (2014b) *Social Work Skills: A Practice Handbook*. Maidenhead: Open University Press.

Turner, V. (1987) *'Betwixt and Between': The Liminal Period in Rites of Passage*. London: Open Court Publishing.

United Nations (1989) *Convention on the Rights of the Child*. Geneva: United Nations.

UN General Assembly (1989) Convention on the Rights of the Child, United Nations, *Treaty Series*, vol. *1577*: 3. Available at: www.refworld.org/docid/3ae6b38f0.html (accessed 2 January 2019).

Viscott, D. (2003) *Finding Your Strength in Difficult Times: A Book of Meditations*. New York: McGraw-Hill.

Vygotsky, L.S. (1978) *Mind in Society: The Development of Higher Psychological Processes*. Cambridge, MA: Harvard University Press.

Vygotsky, L. (2004) Imagination and creativity in childhood. *Journal of Russian and East European Psychology 42*(1): 7–97.

Webb, J., Schirato, T. and Danaher, G. (2002) *Understanding Bourdieu*. London: Sage.

Weick, A. (1983) A growth-task model of human development. *Social Casework 64*(3): 131–7.

Whittaker, A. and Havard, T. (2016) Defensive practice as 'fear-based' practice: Social work's open secret? *British Journal of Social Work 46*(5): 1158–74.

Wieninger, J. (2000) Klientenzentrierte Gesprächsführung. In Bauer, R. and Jehl, R. (eds) *Humanistische Pflege in Theorie und Praxis*. Stuttgart: Schattauer Verlag.

Williams, H.A. (1995) There are no free gifts! Social support and the need for reciprocity. *Human Organization 54*(4): 401–9.

Williams, V. (2018a) *Getting Things Changed: Final Report Summary*. Available at: www.bristol.ac.uk/media-library/sites/sps/images/gettingthingschanged/easy-info/Easy%20read%20Summary%20Full%20Report_web.pdf.

Williams, V. (2018b) How to make people with a learning disability feel more included in society. Available at: https://theconversation.com/how-to-make-people-with-learning-disabilities-feel-more-included-in-society-98493.

Wood, D., Bruner, J. and Ross, G. (1976) The role of tutoring in problem solving. *Journal of Child Psychology and Child Psychiatry 17*(2): 89–100.

Worrall-Davies, A. (2008) Barriers and facilitators to children's and young people's views affecting CAMHS planning and delivery. *Child and Adolescent Mental Health 13*(1): 16–18.

Wright, C. (2012) Plato's just state. Available at: https://philosophynow.org/issues/90/Platos_Just_State.

Wyness, M. (2006) *Childhood and Society: An Introduction to the Sociology of Childhood*. Basingstoke: Palgrave Macmillan.

Wyness, M. (2013) Global standards and deficit childhoods: The contested meaning of children's participation. *Children's Geographies 11*(3): 340–53.

Youth Justice Board (2014) AssetPlus: assessment and planning in the youth justice system. Available at: www.gov.uk/government/publications/assetplus-assessment-and-planning-in-the-youth-justice-system/assetplus-assessment-and-planning-in-the-youth-justice-system.

INDEX

NOTE: page numbers in *italic type* refer to tables and figures.